The

NAPA MURDER

of

ANITA FAGIANI ANDREWS

[signature]

The

NAPA MURDER

of

ANITA FAGIANI ANDREWS

A Cold Case that Caught a Serial Killer

RAYMOND A. GUADAGNI

THE
History
PRESS

Published by The History Press
Charleston, SC
www.historypress.com

Front cover, clockwise from top left: View of Main and Third Streets, Napa, 1970s. *Courtesy of the Napa County Historical Society*; victim Anita Fagiani Andrews. *Courtesy of the Napa County District Attorney's Office*; Napa Valley vineyard. *Photo by Raymond A. Guadagni*; the iconic Fagiani's sign, before it was removed for the major remodel by the new owner in approximately 2015. *Photo by Raymond A. Guadagni*.
Back cover, bottom: Police photo, July 11, 1974, showing the victim's arm as she was found on the blood-soaked floor of the storage room. *Courtesy of the Napa County District Attorney's Office*; top: Roy Melanson mug shot, 1975. *Courtesy of the Napa County District Attorney's Office*.

First published 2021

Manufactured in the United States

ISBN 9781467147415

Library of Congress Control Number: 2020944243

DEDICATION

The events described in this book cover a period of thirty-seven years. Throughout that time, from 1974 to 2011, the work of the Napa Police Department officers exemplified their dedication, devotion and perseverance. Even though they were investigating a seemingly unsolvable case with no obvious suspect and no motive, they never gave up. These professional officers chased every lead, preserved every bit of evidence and spent countless hours working to solve the murder of Anita Andrews.

With the advancement in scientific techniques and the assignment of the case to Detective Don Winegar, and eventually the addition of District Attorney Paul Gero and Investigator Leslie Severe, the murder was finally solved, and the perpetrator was brought to trial.

This book is dedicated to those Napa police officers, and to capable police officers everywhere, for their hard work, for the emotional toll they pay and for how much they care about ensuring that justice is ultimately served.

CONTENTS

Dedication   5
Acknowledgements   9

1. Napa 1974   11
2. The Fagiani Family   14
3. Wednesday, July 10, 1974   18
4. "Woman Found Murdered in Family's Downtown Bar"   24
5. A Criminalist Is Called In   30
6. Investigate Everything   42
7. The Victim's Tan 1967 Cadillac   53
8. Problems   57
9. The Case Goes Cold   60
10. Scientific Advances   62
11. Detective Don Winegar Takes on the Anita Andrews Murder   65
12. Don Winegar Begins Investigation of the Murder   67
13. We Have a Suspect   70
14. A Trial Team Is Formed   73
15. The Interview with the Suspect   78
16. The Photo Lineup   85
17. Who Was Roy Melanson?   90
18. The *Case of People vs. Roy Allen Melanson* Goes to Court   98
19. Before the Trial   101
20. A Surprise Witness   107

CONTENTS

21. The Trial Begins, September 21, 2011   110
22. Testimonies of Those First on the Murder Scene,
     September 21, 2011   115
23. More Incriminating Evidence Is Presented,
     September 22, 2011   122
24. DNA Evidence, September 22 and 23, 2011   132
25. The Jury Visits the Murder Scene at Fagiani's Bar,
     September 23, 2011   139
26. Testimony Continues, September 26, 2011   143
27. Evidence of Past Crimes, September 27, 2011   158
28. Closing Arguments, September 29, 2011   171
29. Jury Deliberations and the Verdict   182
30. Sentencing, Thursday, October 27, 2011   185
31. When a Murder Is Committed   188
32. Where Are They Now?   192

Author's Note   199
Bibliography   201
About the Author   205

ACKNOWLEDGEMENTS

I have received valuable help from many people in writing this book. First and foremost, I thank my wife, Ann, who provided assistance, suggestions and support and sacrificed both time and effort in this endeavor. She has always been my rock (and the rock for our entire family), and she graciously gave both her attention and her energy because she knew it was important to me. Without her, the book would not have been written.

Detective Don Winegar has been incredibly generous in furnishing me with his recollections, materials and timelines from the investigation as well as sharing countless communications during completion of this book. Don's contributions far outweigh any expression of gratitude I could offer him.

Thanks also to trial attorneys Paul Gero and Allison Wilensky, both of whom were tremendously cooperative, and to Investigator Leslie Severe, whose willingness to help went above and beyond. Leslie supplied many photographs and other materials used during the research on this book.

I am indebted to editor Carolyn Woolston, who is a superior wordsmith. Her suggestions were thoughtful and pertinent. On top of that, through this experience Ann and I made a new friend.

My sincere thanks to Todd Shulman of the Napa Police Department; to Kristen Wells at Stanford University, who supplied essential information about DNA testing; to court reporters Michelle Corrigan and Karen Kronquest for sorting through and supplying me with requested trial transcripts; and to friends who served as manuscript beta readers: Mary

Butler, Laura Gorjance and Randy Snowden. I deeply appreciate your time and effort spent on my behalf.

I also want to thank the many people who willingly shared both their recollections of that fateful evening in 1974 and their memories of its effect on the small community of Napa at that time.

1

NAPA 1974

I n 1974, Napa was a bucolic blue-collar town, where many locals worked in the agricultural industry. Almost everyone who lived in Napa worked in town, so there were few commuters other than to nearby Vallejo, a larger city about thirteen miles south that drew many Napans for work at Mare Island Naval Shipyard. Many of the nonagricultural workers were employed by Napa State Hospital or Kaiser Steel Fabrication Plant in Napa. There was very little tourism.

The population was predominantly Caucasian. African American, Asian and Hispanic residents represented a small portion of the total. Most migrant agricultural workers came for the grape harvest and then returned to Mexico or moved on to work the crops in other locales. There were very few good restaurants, and you had to travel out of town to see a play or hear a concert. Kids and teenagers complained there was nothing to do.

At the same time, the community was experiencing significant growth. Redevelopment was underway, and many older buildings were being razed and replaced with modern structures complemented by artwork, clock towers, attractive benches and brick walkways. Concerted efforts were being made to modernize the town and make it more attractive for downtown businesses. City Councilman James V. Jones remembered it this way: "In many ways, things didn't seem much changed from the forties; when the sun went down, they rolled up the sidewalks."

Napa was considered a safe community. Many residents didn't lock their homes or their cars, and most people knew their neighbors. You couldn't walk anywhere in town without someone recognizing you and stopping to talk. Criminal activity was minimal, with few crimes other than alcohol-related offenses—usually bar fights or driving under the influence of alcohol. There were very few armed robberies, murders, narcotics offenses, gang activity or reported sexual assaults.

Law enforcement described Napa as a whiskey- and beer-drinking town; there were twenty-one bars in the city and several just outside city limits. In 1972, twenty deaths in the county were caused by DUI drivers. Drunks were responsible for most of the assaults, stabbings and bar fights, as well. Napa police officer Ronald Hess recalled many a busy graveyard shift, often leaving the station at 11:00 p.m. with lights and siren, driving from bar fight to bar fight. In those days, the police didn't wear bulletproof vests, but they all wore blue-and-white riot helmets.

The intersection of Main and Third Streets marked the southwest corner of downtown Napa. The Conner Hotel stood on the east side of Main. Officer Hess succinctly described the Conner as a "flophouse." On the ground floor of the Conner was the OK Corral bar, and across the street was Fagiani's Cocktail Lounge, which the police regarded as a bar for old-timer drinkers. The Gilt Edge and the Oberon were located just up the block at

View of Main Street at Third Street, Napa, depicting Fagiani's Cocktail Lounge, the Plaza Hotel and other local downtown businesses in the 1970s. *Courtesy of the Napa County Historical Society.*

View of Main Street at First Street, Napa, two blocks north of Fagiani's Cocktail Lounge, as it appeared in the 1970s. *Courtesy of the Napa County Historical Society.*

Main and Second. One street over on Brown Street was the Plaza Hotel and Bar, which was a quieter lounge, though it, too, had its lively nights.

O'Sullivan's was situated on First Street at Juarez; the Aquarius was downtown on First, and Mike's Club was nearby on Coombs Street. Don's was located at Third Street, where it dead-ended (at that time) at Soscol Avenue. The Depot, Red Carpet, Night Cap and Napa Bowl (which had its own bar and its own troubles) were strung along Soscol. Jack's Club, at Soscol and Silverado Trail, was the dedicated-drinker spot. On the north end of town, Trancas Street, with its collection of drinking establishments, was a world of its own.

Alcohol-related arrests were common, often for the simple offense of being drunk in public. According to Officer Hess, "The next time you met a person whom you'd arrested for bar fighting or on a DUI, they would apologize."

There was no Public Defender's Office at that time; the crime rate simply did not warrant one. If a criminal defendant could not afford to retain counsel, the judge appointed a local lawyer from a rotating list of attorneys, even though few of these appointed attorneys had criminal defense experience.

In 1974, Napa was still a small town, a pleasant place to live, work and raise a family.

2

THE FAGIANI FAMILY

Anita Fagiani Andrews's father, Nick Fagiani, owned the well-known Fagiani's Cocktail Lounge. Her uncle Andrew Fagiani was a Napa County supervisor. Muriel Fagiani, her sister, was a schoolteacher known as the watchdog of local government because she regularly attended meetings of the Napa City Council, County Board of Supervisors and the local school board. Anita was a longtime secretary at Napa State Hospital.

Nick Fagiani opened his bar in 1945 and ran it until his death in 1969, when his daughters inherited it. To retain the valuable liquor license issued by the Alcoholic Beverage Commission to their father, the sisters continued to operate the bar. The license allowed sale of alcohol to bar patrons as well as to customers purchasing alcohol to take off-premises. Thus, Fagiani's was both a bar and a liquor store, and it was called, appropriately, Fagiani's Cocktail Lounge and Liquor Store.

Those on-site/off-site liquor sale licenses were valid as long as the bar continued to operate, but if it closed for a six-month period, the license would be terminated and could not be reissued. Both sisters were determined to keep the bar open. Because they couldn't afford to hire staff, they agreed to alternate shifts as bartender during evenings and on weekends, even though they both had day jobs.

Anita Fagiani was popular growing up. As an eighteen-year-old, she was chosen Miss Napa County. At the time of her death, she was fifty-one years old and divorced, with two daughters. For a number of years, she had a boyfriend, but they had broken up shortly before her death.

Murder victim Anita Fagiani Andrews (*left*) with her father, Nicola, and sister, Muriel. *Courtesy of the Napa County District Attorney's Office.*

Anita dressed well and enjoyed accessorizing with jewelry. She was neat and fastidious, a person of set habits and routines to which she adhered faithfully. She always opened the bar around 5:00 p.m. after getting off work at Napa State Hospital, and she closed up between 9:00 p.m. and 11:00 p.m., depending on how many customers were present. There were usually few patrons, so ordinarily she was able to lock up around 10:00 p.m.

At the start of each evening, Anita parked her 1967 Cadillac in front of the bar, unlocked the padlock on the front door and switched on the neon light to signal that Fagiani's was open. In small towns like Napa, the police know a lot about the local business owners and their habits. They knew Fagiani's was now owned by the two sisters and that there were no employees. Napa police were also aware that the two women alternated shifts and only one

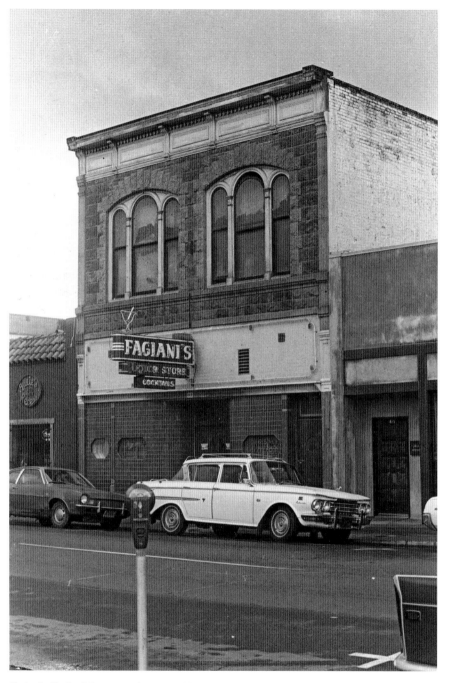

Fagiani's Cocktail Lounge as it appeared in the 1970s. *Courtesy of the Napa County Historical Society.*

was on duty at any given time. And they knew Fagiani's catered to mostly male patrons in a not-so-nice part of town.

Patrol officers had a routine for checking on the bar. The officer on duty on a given evening would drive down Main Street to see if Anita's Cadillac was parked in front. He would shine his spotlight on the front door. If the padlock was unlocked and the outside light on, he would assume the bar was open and everything was fine. However, if the Cadillac was *not* parked in front, the door was padlocked, the outside light was out and only an interior light was showing, it meant the bar was not open and no one was inside. This informal routine had worked well for the five years since the sisters had taken over the bar.

But on the night of the murder, it happened that the patrol officer did not follow the usual routine. If he had, he would have noticed something suspicious: the padlock on the front door was unlocked, but the Cadillac was gone. That might have led the officer to check inside the bar and immediately discover Anita's body. In that case, law enforcement could potentially have gained a substantially greater head-start in searching for the Cadillac, increasing the odds of locating the car and identifying the murderer.

Instead, thirty-seven years would pass, and the killer would commit more murders before he was finally apprehended and brought to justice.

3

WEDNESDAY, JULY 10, 1974

The number one topic of discussion around the town of Napa during the week of July 10, 1974, was what Mayor Ralph Bolin called "an unseasonable rainstorm." Although the rain eased the fire danger from the intense July heat, when the storm hit it played havoc on the City Police Department since its new building, then under construction, had no roof. No one expected rain in the Napa Valley during July.

July evenings in Napa are usually warm, and that Wednesday evening was no exception. The temperature hovered in the high seventies. At Kiwanis Park, several blocks south of downtown, teams of teenage girls were playing fast-pitch softball. Across the river to the east, high school boys played baseball under the lights at the Napa fairgrounds ballpark. The Uptown Theatre was showing *The Great Gatsby*, starring Robert Redford and Mia Farrow.

None of that mattered to Al Mufich, Al Mackenzie or David Luce as they strolled down Third Street to the Happy Hours bar, one of their favorite hangouts, to grab a beer and chat. Next, they intended to visit Catania's Pizza Parlor on Silverado Trail, where Al Mackenzie was playing steel guitar in the band.

Mackenzie was personable, smart and fun to be around, a happy, playful man who liked to enjoy himself. Luce enjoyed his friends and liked sharing beers with them. Mufich, as later described by David Luce, was "a bit odd. He was older than we were, had a full beard with shoulder-length white hair and was eccentric. Sometimes his behavior could be pretty strange. He

Recent photo of the restored Uptown Theatre on Third Street, several blocks west of Fagiani's Cocktail Lounge. *Photo by Raymond A. Guadagni.*

could be loud, boisterous, belligerent and abusive. Al was a Napa native, so he knew everything about everybody."

After a few rounds of beer, the three men left Happy Hours and made their way down Third to Main Street. They still had some time before Mackenzie's musical performance, and as they neared the corner, they decided to add a stop at Fagiani's Cocktail Lounge. When one entered Fagiani's through the front door, the wooden bar ran along the left wall, with stools all the way down toward the back of the room. A pool table sat in the middle of the room. Along the opposite wall were a few tables with chairs and a jukebox. Three taxidermy deer heads looked down on the scene. At the end of the bar was a small storage room for supplies. A staircase led to offices upstairs. Even in 1974, the bar looked like something out of an earlier era. The beautiful, old-fashioned countertop had a backdrop of mirrors and a colorful array of liquor bottles; the basic commercial pool table with its green felt top appeared to have been heavily used over the years. The barstools were old but in fair condition, and the tables across from the bar showed wear.

The three friends arrived at Fagiani's around 9:00 p.m., settling on the three stools closest to the front door. Al Mufich sat nearest the entrance,

Police photo taken inside Fagiani's Cocktail Lounge on July 11, 1974, showing the front entrance, bar and pool table. *Courtesy of the Napa County District Attorney's Office.*

Police photo taken inside Fagiani's Cocktail Lounge on July 11, 1974, showing pool table, jukebox, taxidermy deer heads and customer table. *Courtesy of the Napa County District Attorney's Office.*

Police photo taken inside Fagiani's Cocktail Lounge on July 11, 1974, showing the back end of the bar and the door to the storage room. *Courtesy of the Napa County District Attorney's Office.*

and David Luce sat in the middle with Al Mackenzie on Luce's right. Sitting close to the front door was intentional. "When I go into a bar," Luce explained, "I survey the entire inside to see who's there and where they are, because things happen in bars, fracases occur, and you have to know where all the players are."

As the three friends settled in, they noticed a man sitting on a barstool toward the back of the room. "The bartender lady was standing across from him behind the counter," Luce recalled. The man was angled on his stool so he faced away from the three at the front, and when the friends ordered their beers they noticed something: the man was covering his face, as if shielding himself from view. According to Luce, "His hand was out away from his head a few inches sideways but not touching his head." He had an ashtray in front of him and was smoking a cigarette and drinking a beer. Nothing was remarkable about his clothing; he wore an inexpensive shirt, unbuttoned at the neck with the lapels flat open. He was Caucasian and looked to be in his forties.

The possibility that the man was intentionally covering his face did not sit well with Al Mufich. He yelled, "Hey, you son of a bitch, what are you hiding from? Why are you hiding your face?"

Luce and Mackenzie were concerned that Mufich might get thrown out of the bar, and since he'd already been banned for life from several other bars, they didn't want him to be permanently barred from another establishment. Believing this was not going to end well, Luce pleaded with Mufich to stop yelling.

"I don't care," Mufich said. But he did stop yelling.

The man at the back of the bar seemed oblivious, showing no reaction to Mufich's yelling, and the three friends resumed sipping their beer. As they got ready to leave, Luce decided to go to the bathroom. He had another motive as well; he wanted to make sure everything was okay with the stranger.

On his way back from the men's room, he stopped at the man's stool and said, "Hey, don't get too excited about Al." Then he stuck his hand out. The stranger took his hand and shook it. Then Luce turned to Anita Fagiani Andrews, the bartender that night, and asked if the man was her boyfriend. She said he was. Luce then rejoined his two friends at the opposite end of the bar.

Luce later said he didn't recall any conversation between himself and the stranger, but he did remember something significant about the handshake. "It was hot, soft and wimpy, like there were no bones in his hand." Luce, a construction worker, had rough, calloused hands.

He said he would never forget that handshake. Only once before had he encountered one like it—years earlier, in Alaska, he'd shaken Richard Nixon's hand. He said it was the same hot, soft handshake he'd experienced with this stranger. Luce later estimated that his total contact with the man amounted to about twenty to thirty seconds.

After finishing their beers, Luce and his buddies left Fagiani's. They had been at the bar for approximately half an hour. No one else came in while they were there. When they left, there were only two people at Fagiani's: the bartender and the stranger.

Anita Fagiani Andrews was never seen alive again.

4

"WOMAN FOUND MURDERED IN FAMILY'S DOWNTOWN BAR"

Napa Register, Thursday, July 11, 1974

It is of paramount importance to solve serious crimes quickly, particularly a homicide. According to former Napa police chief Steve Potter, "If a murder is not solved within the first forty-eight hours, the chance that it will ever be solved diminishes in direct proportion to the time that passes."

Rapid results can only be the product of immediate and intensive investigation, which explains why, when detectives are called to a murder scene, they often work around the clock. It doesn't matter to the police if it is day or night; they will work the crime scene continuously until it has been completely processed. That processing includes attention to even the most minuscule fleck of blood or hair that seems out of place. Of course, if the murder occurred at night, they might have to wait until sunrise to detect all the evidence, but they are fully aware that they are working against an invisible stopwatch, mocking them as it tick-tocks the time away and the killer's advantage grows. But as unimaginable as it might sound, in this instance it took law enforcement thirty-seven years to solve the case.

On Thursday, July 11, 1974, at around 8:40 a.m., Muriel Fagiani received a phone call from her mother, who reported that Anita had not arrived for work at the Napa State Hospital that morning. Muriel told her mother she would try to locate her sister. She then drove to the bar, walked

Woman Found Murdered In Family's Downtown Bar

By JOHN GREEN, Register Staff Writer

A 31-year-old Napa woman was found raped and murdered in the back room of a downtown bar this morning.

She was identified as Anita Elizabeth Andrews of 2801 Soscol Ave. discovered sprawled on the floor of the room with her throat slashed.

The discovery was made by the victim's younger sister, Muriel Fagiani, around 9 a.m. For years a family enterprise, the sisters jointly operated the bar, called Fagiani's Cocktail Lounge and Liquor Store and located at 813 Main St. The victim was also employed at Napa State Hospital.

Police said they believed the incident occurred sometime during the night. The victim reportedly had been working the 1 p.m. to 9 p.m. shift at the bar on Wednesday.

Authorities issued an all points bulletin in their search for the victim's car, which was missing from the spot where it normally was parked in front of the bar.

The car was described as a 1967 model tan-colored Cadillac with license numbers UGA 370.

"It would appear that the car is missing," District Attorney James D. Boitano told the Register on the scene this morning. "If anybody sees it, they should report it to the Napa Police Department. Anyone who finds it should not touch it. They should not do anything to it."

"We've skimmed the whole neighborhood," said Boitano, "in case she changed her pattern and parked somewhere else, but the car is not here."

Chief of Police Jennings and his detectives swarmed around the bar this morning to begin their investigation of the incident, which is the sixth homicide to occur in Napa County this year.

Boitano said he had ordered an autopsy and called in criminologist Peter Barnett of Berkeley to aid in the investigation.

Barnett, according to Boitano, "might very well tell us a lot and we obviously don't want to tamper with the scene until he gets a shot at it."

The body had not been removed from the bar at 10:30 a.m. today.

The victim's sister told investigators she had found the bar's front door open when she

(Continued on Page 2)

The Napa Register

112th Year, No. 282 — Thursday, July 11, 1974 — Price: 10 Cents

Impeachment Probe

Nixon's Fear—Exposure

WASHINGTON (UPI) — President Nixon expressed fear in the early stages of the Watergate investigation that his early actions would be... ment inquiry evidence published Thursday.

The committee released eight volumes of accumulated evidence and documentation about... Most of the material, which weighed several pounds, was carefully documented compilation of information already in... —On June 20, 1972 less than two weeks after the Watergate burglary, Nixon expressed the fear that his inquiry would lead beyond House to the President. And —On March 17, 1973, as the investigation intensified, Nixon expressed the fear that his top aides the would lead "to the White House"...

A GRIEF-STRICKEN Muriel Fagiani talks to District Attorney James D. Boitano this morning outside the bar where her sister was discovered murdered. The victim was Anita Elizabeth Andrews, 31, of 2601 Soscol Ave., who with her sister operated the bar and liquor store at 813 Main St. (Register Photo by Bob McKenzie)

Napa Register front page, July 11, 1974: "Woman Found Murdered in Family's Downtown Bar." *Napa County Newspaper Archive.*

in and discovered Anita's body in the storage room. She immediately called the police.

Napa Register journalist John Green and his photographer, Bob McKenzie, were nearby in Bob's car, following up on a story they had been covering. Bob had a police scanner in his car, and while they were en route to their assignment, they heard a police dispatcher announce on the scanner a possible homicide at 813 Main Street, Fagiani's Cocktail Lounge. When they heard the call, they were only a block away, so they turned around and drove straight to the bar.

They arrived close to 9:00 a.m., even before the police arrived. The bar door was wide open. They went in and found Muriel Fagiani standing near the front of the bar. She appeared to be in a state of shock. She said to John, "That's my sister lying over there."

Bob and John decided they should go outside to wait for the police. John later said the bar was "dark inside," that he was inside only briefly and didn't see anyone else either inside the bar or outside.

Officer Joe Moore, who was on duty that day, heard a patrol call go out to Officer Robert Boals indicating that he had a coroner's case on Main Street. Boals wasn't available, so Moore took the call and proceeded to Fagiani's bar, arriving at about 9:05 a.m. He was the first police officer on the scene. He proceeded into the bar through the front door, saw Muriel

Police photo, July 11, 1974, depicting blood spatter in storage room where the victim's body was found. *Courtesy of the Napa County District Attorney's Office.*

Fagiani standing at the far end of the bar and walked over to her. She appeared to be calm and said, "I think my sister's been raped, and she's in there." Moore later said he believed Muriel's outwardly calm demeanor was due to shock.

Muriel opened the door to the back storage room and turned on the light. On the floor just inside the door lay the body of her sister, Anita Fagiani. It was a brutal murder. Anita had been beaten, stabbed multiple times through the neck and torso with a screwdriver and sexually assaulted. Moore, who did not know the deceased, saw an adult Caucasian female, her clothing torn and in disarray, with blood around her upper torso area and on the floor. He first checked the victim's carotid artery for a pulse but detected no sign of life. The officer and Muriel then moved out of the storage room and turned off the light. Moore urged Muriel to move to the front door so he could secure the crime scene, but she did not want to leave her sister. He stayed with her until additional police officers arrived,

Police photo, July 11, 1974, showing the victim's arm as she was found on the blood-soaked floor of the storage room. *Courtesy of the Napa County District Attorney's Office.*

including Captain Dewey Burnsed, Lieutenant John Bailey and Sergeant Don Kemper. Together, they convinced Muriel to leave the bar. Officer Moore put her in his patrol car and stayed with her. No one else came to the scene other than those who were there on official business, including other police officers, District Attorney James D. Boitano and Deputy District Attorney John Cooley.

The investigators took charge of the scene, and Officer Moore returned to patrol. Within an hour, Moore received a dispatcher's call to contact a David Luce at the Happy Hours bar on Third Street. He found Luce at the bar at about 10:30 a.m. and interviewed him there.

Napa police lieutenant John Bailey arrived at Fagiani's at about 9:10 a.m. and was assigned to lead the investigation. He was well qualified for the job. Besides being an experienced investigator, he had spent twelve years as a patrol officer assigned to the beat that included Fagiani's. He estimated that in an eight-hour beat he might drive by the bar three, four or even five times.

Right: Napa police captain Dewey Burnsed. *Below, left*: Napa police sergeant Don Kemper. *Below, right*: Napa police sergeant Charles Hansen. *Courtesy of the Napa Police Historical Society.*

Bailey's first act was to clear the building interior and take control of access. He assigned the crime scene investigation over to Sergeant Chuck Hansen and began to search for Anita's missing 1967 Cadillac, starting at the victim's apartment in north Napa. When the car was not found anywhere in town, he put out an all-points bulletin (APB) on the car for the city and the state.

5

A CRIMINALIST IS CALLED IN

The Napa Police Department had no consulting criminalist, no crime scene reconstructionist and no laboratory. It did have a small office for processing fingerprints, and it had Police Sergeant Chuck Hansen, a skilled de facto criminalist, although he had no formal training in forensics. On the morning the victim was discovered, District Attorney James Boitano immediately called in a Bay Area licensed criminalist, Peter D. Barnett, to collect, preserve and process evidence and to perform a crime scene reconstruction.

Boitano was a frugal man. Some said he still had the first nickel he ever earned, and he was frugal with his budget, as well. But he spared no expense in hiring a private criminalist who had previously qualified numerous times as an expert witness in a wide range of criminal cases.

The task of the criminalist is to assess the scene of an incident that may result in litigation. Whether a crime or an accident, the criminalist's job is to document the scene and collect and preserve any physical evidence that may help explain what happened. The criminalist collects evidence, which is then sent to the laboratory, where specific experiments are performed and tests conducted to understand how that physical evidence came to be and what it reveals about an event. The criminalist produces a report, which is usually used in testimony during a trial to explain how the evidence was collected, documented and analyzed. When there are no known suspects, no motive, no witnesses and few answers, the criminalist may also do a crime scene reconstruction, the goal being to use the available evidence to determine the most likely combination of actions and timelines giving rise to the crime.

Left: Napa police chief Ken Jennings. *Right*: Napa police detective Ron Montgomery. *Courtesy of the Napa Police Historical Society.*

Barnett arrived at the crime scene at 10:30 a.m. on July 11, 1974, and immediately spoke with Police Chief Ken Jennings, Sergeant Hansen, Detective Ron Montgomery, District Attorney Boitano, Deputy District Attorney John Cooley and Muriel Fagiani, sister of the decedent.

After that, he walked through the scene of the murder, accompanied by Muriel Fagiani, to identify anything that was out of place or that she didn't recognize as belonging in the bar. When Muriel left, Barnett and Sergeant Hansen continued to process the scene and collect physical evidence, inspecting each room in the bar looking for any evidence of what had occurred the previous evening, in particular, blood, damaged areas or anything that was out of place or unusual. They also documented the scene with photographs and notes, in addition to chalk lines outlining the victim's body.

The collected evidence was then transported to the laboratory for analysis. Barnett also documented other aspects of the scene pertinent to reconstruction of the crime. Measurements and photographs were taken, and diagrams were drawn in specific areas of concern. He noted that the bar countertop looked as if it had been recently cleaned. Towel wipe marks were still observable on the counter surface, and toward the back end of the bar there was an ashtray containing a cigarette butt.

Police photo, July 11, 1974, of the chalk outline of the victim's body on the floor of the storage room. *Courtesy of the Napa County District Attorney's Office.*

Police photo, July 11, 1974, of the bartender's work area behind the bar. *Courtesy of the Napa County District Attorney's Office.*

Police photo, July 11, 1974. All of the barstools were lined up neatly with one exception: the stool of the last customer in the bar that night, who also left a cigarette butt in an ashtray. *Courtesy of the Napa County District Attorney's Office.*

Opposite, top: Police photo, July 11, 1974. A screwdriver was found on the drainboard next to the sink, and a single ashtray with a cigarette butt remained on the bar. *Courtesy of the Napa County District Attorney's Office.*

Opposite, bottom: Police photo, July 11, 1974. The screwdriver was the presumed murder weapon. *Courtesy of the Napa County District Attorney's Office.*

Above: Police photo, July 11, 1974. A bloody towel was found on the floor under the sink. *Courtesy of the Napa County District Attorney's Office.*

Barnett also observed that the stools were neatly arranged along the bar as one might leave them when closing for the night, with one exception: one stool had been moved out from the bar and was sitting at an angle, and that stool was next to the ashtray found on the counter.

Behind the bar, Barnett noted a sink close to the location of the ashtray. This area appeared clean and neat, with everything in its place, except for a screwdriver on the drain board. He picked it up and noticed a rust stain underneath the shaft where it had been sitting on the metal drain board. He also noted the rust stain corresponded to the side of the screwdriver that had been resting on the drain board. To Barnett, this indicated the screwdriver had been placed on the drain when it was wet or when the sink was wet or both. He concluded that rust had developed where water would have remained between the round screwdriver shaft and the sink surface.

Barnett then conducted a test for presumptive blood in the sink and found a small amount. He also found a towel on the floor beneath the sink. It was dry, but stiff and crumpled, suggesting it had been dropped on the floor while wet and had remained there until it had dried.

Finally, Barnett took approximately eighty photographs of the crime scene. In addition to photographs taken in the bar, including the ashtray, cigarette butt, towel, washcloth and rum and beer bottles, he photographed the victim as well as other items found in the storage room.

The victim was lying on the floor on her back with her feet toward the door. She was partially unclothed. There was extensive pooling of blood on the floor and blood spatters in various areas on the inside of the storage room, on the walls and on objects in the room. On the floor near the body was a shoe, one or two buttons and an earring.

The state of the victim's clothing spoke of a struggle with her assailant. She was wearing pantyhose under a pair of slacks, and the slacks were

Above: Police photo, July 11, 1974. Blood spatter in the storage room where the victim's body was found. *Courtesy of the Napa County District Attorney's Office.*

Opposite, top: Police photo, July 11, 1974. The brutal murder resulted in blood throughout the storage room. *Courtesy of the Napa County District Attorney's Office.*

Opposite, bottom: Police photo, July 11, 1974. Blood spatter in the storage room. *Courtesy of the Napa County District Attorney's Office.*

entirely off her right leg but still on her left leg. One of her shoes was on; the other shoe was off. One shoe had a torn piece of the pantyhose in it. The victim's blouse had been opened completely and her brassiere pulled down, exposing her breasts. She was wearing panties and a girdle, both of which had been removed from her right leg. Her genital area was exposed.

Barnett also observed broken glass in the storage room; the fragments appeared to be from a soft drink bottle. A jagged portion of the bottle lay on the floor near the body. Glass fragments were also found on the victim's clothing and in her hair. Barnett collected blood samples from the scene and lifted impressions of the footprints he saw. Then he examined the staircase leading up to Fagiani's business office. He found bloodstains on the fourth, sixth, eighth and tenth steps.

Barnett entered the business office, which was in a state of disarray. A search for Anita's purse, pocketbook or credit cards was fruitless. They were never found.

That same afternoon, Barnett observed and photographed the postmortem examination performed by the coroner, Dr. David Clary. He

Police photo, July 11, 1974. Broken glass was found near the victim's body in the storage room. *Courtesy of the Napa County District Attorney's Office.*

Police photo, July 11, 1974. A bottle was found on the stairs leading to the upstairs office of the bar. *Courtesy of the Napa County District Attorney's Office.*

Above: Police photo, July 11, 1974. The cashbox in the upstairs office was apparently ransacked by the killer. *Courtesy of the Napa County District Attorney's Office.*

Left: Police photo, July 11, 1974. The cashbox in the upstairs office was empty of money. *Courtesy of the Napa County District Attorney's Office.*

also took her fingerprints and collected fingernail clippings. Then he took the screwdriver, the victim's clothing and other items of evidence back to his laboratory for processing. He hoped the evidence would provide a viable connection to a suspect.

6

INVESTIGATE EVERYTHING

By the end of the day after the body was discovered, the police had interviewed Muriel Fagiani and David Luce, spent hours investigating the crime scene and brought in a criminalist to collect detailed physical evidence and develop a crime scene reconstruction. Now they were faced with the daunting and sometimes tedious task of running down every possible lead, no matter how farfetched.

Detectives endeavored to contact everyone they could locate who had known Anita Andrews. Investigators began by interviewing Anita's daughters, Diana and Donna. Then they interviewed Anita's friends. She had lived in Napa her entire life, so dozens of people were interviewed. No one could recall any problem or significant disagreement Anita might have had with anyone. She had no financial troubles and had never mentioned any threat being made against her.

From the outset of the investigation, police attention was drawn to the Conner Hotel, a run-down hotel directly across the street from Fagiani's bar. Many of its residents were mentally ill individuals who had been released from the state hospital system by Governor Ronald Reagan in the late 1960s and were living on subsidies from the county. Other resident boarders were Vietnam War veterans suffering from posttraumatic stress disorder.

When the police interviewed Mary Vacarella, the hotel manager, she told them that shortly after 10:00 p.m. on the evening of the murder, she had looked out the window facing Fagiani's bar and observed that the lights were on. However, she did not see Anita's Cadillac. This was unusual because it

The Conner Hotel, directly across Main Street from Fagiani's Cocktail Lounge. The hotel was later demolished as part of redevelopment. The site is now a city park. *Napa County Newspaper Archive.*

was not consistent with Anita's customary routine: if her car was gone, it meant Anita was gone, too. The police asked Vacarella to go through the registration cards for the hotel and said they would check back with her later.

A man named Elenes Feliciano, a resident at the Conner Hotel, was interviewed by the police. He admitted to being in Fagiani's bar twice on the day of the murder. The first time was around 4:45 p.m. During that visit, he saw Anita tending bar and noticed only one other male customer. When he returned at 7:15 p.m., Anita was still bartending, but a different male customer was in the bar. Feliciano offered to buy Anita and this man a drink. Anita declined, but the man accepted his offer and had a beer. Feliciano could only describe this man as having a southern accent, possibly Texan, and wearing a short-sleeved shirt. At some point during this second visit, Feliciano was joined in the bar by Mary Norton, also a resident at the Conner Hotel. Feliciano stayed in the bar for approximately forty-five minutes on this visit. He and Norton left together at approximately 8:00 p.m.

When interviewed by police detectives, Norton confirmed that she had been at Fagiani's in the early evening hours on July 10. She said Anita was tending bar, and there were two customers: Elenes Feliciano and another male. In contrast to Feliciano's vague recollection, Norton's description of that other male was very specific: he was about thirty-eight years old, six feet tall with a long torso and slender build and straight, thinning light brown hair worn short. He had a ruddy complexion and wore a dark-colored jacket, a blue shirt open at the neck, dark pants and brown shoes.

Detectives checked back with Conner Hotel manager Mary Vacarella to learn what she had found in her review of the hotel's registration records. She told them two men had checked in at approximately 11:00 p.m. on July 10. They stayed in room 16 and left very early on the morning of the eleventh. One of these men was a Dave Flores, who gave his address as 1193 Poplar Drive in El Paso, Texas. He was dark complexioned, around thirty years old and wore a black hat. The second man was about six foot one with a husky build, bushy black hair and a dark complexion. Napa police contacted El Paso police detective R. Gonzalez, advised him of the Napa murder investigation and requested information on Dave Flores and any known associates. Detective Gonzalez informed them there was no such address as 1193 Poplar Drive, though there was a Poplar Street. Gonzalez also had no police file on Flores.

Another potential suspect was identified on the day Anita's body was discovered. Liston Casey Beal fit the description of the person last seen talking to the victim in Fagiani's bar the day of the murder. Detectives learned that Beal had been in Napa visiting his ex-wife and daughter and had been staying at the Plaza Hotel at Brown and Second Streets, which was around the corner from Fagiani's. Beal had checked out on July 10. Because of Beal's description and his proximity on the day in question, some members of the investigation team decided he was the killer. That belief survived for more than twenty years.

Because Anita worked in an office at Napa State Hospital, one of the first things the police did was search the entire hospital grounds for her Cadillac, without success. Police also interviewed Arthur Morgan, a program director at the hospital. Morgan said some patients had off-site passes, allowing them to leave the hospital grounds during program hours. He also said that, because of her job duties, Anita had contact with hospital patients. Police asked whether any patients were unaccounted for on the evening of the murder. Morgan checked his records and determined no patients had left the hospital on the evening Anita died.

The police also investigated whether any hospital patients had a history of rape or attacking women by stabbing. They were told of a Clyde Jones who had previously been committed to the hospital and had a history

Mug shot of Liston Beal, one of the early suspects. Some law enforcement officers believed for many years that he was the killer. *Courtesy of the Napa County District Attorney's Office.*

of rapes and stabbings. He was no longer a hospital resident, and his whereabouts required further investigation. Coincidentally, there was also a Clyde Eldon Jones who was on leave from Napa State Hospital and now residing at the Phoenix House, a home in Napa for mentally ill patients deemed stable enough to be released from the state hospital. Police determined that Clyde Eldon Jones had no history of rape or stabbing and concluded that he was not a suspect.

While focusing specifically on violent criminally insane inmates at Napa State Hospital, police learned of a patient named Richard Randall. He had been a patient for two years, but in 1969, prior to his commitment to the hospital, he was placed at Atascadero State Hospital for rape and homicide. Because Randall had a prior history of violence, the investigation briefly focused on him. When he was located, detectives interrogated him, but they ultimately determined that he had nothing to do with Anita's murder.

On the day Anita's murder was discovered, Captain Dewey Burnsed and Lieutenant Robert Jarecki checked Anita's residence on Soscol Avenue, a couple of miles from Fagiani's bar. Her Cadillac was not found, and no signs of disturbance were noted at her apartment. However, they did learn of some possible suspects. Anita lived in apartment 14. Don Orchid and his wife lived in apartment 10, directly below the victim's. Orchid advised Burnsed and Jarecki that Anita had two male friends who visited occasionally. One was Joseph Silva, a fifty-year-old man who was tall and slender with salt-and-pepper hair. They reported that Silva drove a white Cadillac with a AAA sticker on the windshield. The second male friend was described as being six feet tall and forty to fifty years old. They said he drove a 1969 Ford station wagon. This man kept a German shepherd with him all the time.

Interviews with David Luce and Al Mackenzie at the police station on the day following the murder elicited the most detailed description of a potential suspect police were able to obtain at any point during the entire thirty-seven-year investigation. Luce, Mackenzie and Mufich, the three friends who were together in Fagiani's bar on the night of the slaying, described the man they had seen there as fortyish with a wet-head hairstyle, small ears flat to the head and thin lips. He was six feet tall and 175 pounds with long arms and smooth muscles, wearing a short-sleeved blue shirt open at the neck. The men each related to investigators the story of the man covering his face with one hand, Mufich yelling at him and Luce later apologizing to him. Luce also reported asking Anita if the man was her boyfriend and her saying yes. The police determined Luce's description of this unknown person required further investigation.

In any homicide case with a female victim, one of the first suspects police investigate is the victim's husband or ex-husband. Napa police investigators contacted Clarence Andrews, also known as Mike, who was Anita Fagiani Andrews's ex-husband. Mike Andrews ran a charter boat business out of Crockett marina. He told Napa detectives he and Anita had been divorced for about twenty-one years, and while he had not had any direct contact with her for a number of years, he had kept up with her life through their youngest daughter, Donna.

In the article "Napa Bar Is a Reminder of Old Murder" in the November 17, 1989 *San Francisco Chronicle*, staff writer Sam Whiting reported that during the initial investigation in 1974, Mike Andrews provided the police with information he had received from Donna about a man in Anita's life whose first name was Don. He was a mechanic for a carnival, SJM Fiesta Shows, out of Southern California. Mike said that, according to Donna, Anita "had trouble with Don." In fact, during the last telephone conversation Donna had with her mother, Anita told her she was upset with her former boyfriend, who was a repairman for a carnival. "She was really mad because he ran up a four-hundred-dollar phone bill at her apartment. She didn't want to see him anymore, but she had his tools in the back of her car and felt that she had to." For some reason, Donna had not disclosed this during her interview with the investigators.

According to the article, Donna also told her father she believed that if the killer *was* Don, he might have gone to the bar to see Anita about getting his tools and Anita might have told him that before she would give him the tools, he had to pay his $400 debt. That lead looked promising. Apparently, there had also been arguments between Don and Anita over debts he ran up on Anita's credit card. Anita was upset to the extent that she took Don's expensive tools as collateral for what he owed her and kept the tools in the trunk of her Cadillac. But since the Cadillac was missing, there was no way to verify this information.

Whiting's newspaper article also stated that Lieutenant Jarecki and the Napa police believed this was important information they should have been told immediately. According to Jarecki, "It was never relayed to us that the carnival worker was also a welder, or that the carnival worker's tools were in the back of Anita's car." Nor was it known whether Anita had a current relationship with the man. "If this had come out in the investigation," Jarecki later said, "he would have been prime suspect No. 1. We've got to find out where this guy is now."

According to an unidentified witness, there had been a welder or mechanic in the bar on the night of the murder, and police conjectured it was possible this welder and the carnival worker ex-boyfriend were one and the same person. If so, he could be the killer.

The police then decided to re-contact Mike Andrews, Anita's ex-husband, who corroborated his daughter's information. According to Whiting, Andrews stated, "This guy would visit Anita and became more or less a half-ass steady. He fit the description of the suspect perfectly, and he had access to Anita's Cadillac. Then he pulled a disappearing act from the carnival where he worked. This is weird. I mean *weird*."

Following up on this lead, police subsequently learned the man's full name was Don Young, and he was a mechanic. They also learned that Don Young was no longer employed at SJM Fiesta Shows because of a drinking issue. However, according to police records, they ultimately determined that Young was not a viable suspect.

Local bartenders form a community of sorts, especially in a small town. They are usually friendly with one another and communicate about common issues in their business. For example, they might phone a fellow bartender if they see a belligerent drunk leave their bar and possibly head for another. In the course of the investigation, police interviewed local bartenders to learn what they knew about Anita's private life and to identify possible suspects that might require follow-up investigation.

Bartenders Kathy Brown of Hooch House, Mary Ratto of the New Roma and Cliff Kranzler of Cliff's Club were contacted because all three were known to be friends of Anita's. Elmer Jenkins, bartender at the Oberon on Main Street north of Fagiani's, was also contacted. His recollection was he had seen Fagiani's sign turned off around 10:00 or 10:15 p.m., in contrast to other witnesses' reports. Ratto, bartender at the New Roma, said she knew the victim very well. She said that for the two weeks preceding the murder, Anita had been closing Fagiani's early. Anita, Mary and Mary's husband would then meet up at the Gilt Edge and play dice, drink and visit. However, on the night of the murder, Anita did not show up at the Gilt Edge to meet with the Rattos. Mary Ratto felt this was strange. Several other local bartenders were interviewed. Some knew Anita well, but they could provide no useful information.

Joseph Silva was one of the men Anita's neighbor Don Orchid had described to the police. Silva told police he had a couple of conversations with Anita during the two days prior to the crime. On July 8, he called her at the bar and invited her out for dinner. She called him back and took a rain check on dinner. On July 9, Anita visited Silva and his son at their residence at 11:30 p.m. upon her return from a meeting in St. Helena. Silva said Anita did not seem to be upset about anything in particular. That was the last time he ever saw her.

Another friend of Anita's who came to the attention of the police was Melvio P. Milani. During his interview, Milani was visibly upset over Anita's death. He had known her for a number of years, had dated her and at one time had considered marriage. However, Milani was unable to furnish information about any of Anita's recent companions. Later in July, police re-contacted Milani to verify his whereabouts on the day of the murder. He stated he was with a friend in Crockett until 8:45 p.m. that evening and then was at his daughter's house until 10:30 p.m. Milani's alibi was verified. Police determined that further investigation was not warranted.

Investigators also interviewed Jimmie Lee Kidwell, who they learned might have had a relationship with Anita. He told police he had met Anita a few weeks before her murder and had gone out to dinner and drinks with her a few times. However, he had never been in her bar and had never had a physical relationship with her, though he did admit spending one night at her apartment after having had too much to drink. Kidwell knew of no other male acquaintances and could furnish no further information about the crime.

Police contacted Napa resident T.C. Lollis, who had reportedly been in Fagiani's bar on the day of the murder. Lollis said he was there around 4:20 p.m. when the bar opened, and he stayed until 5:10 p.m. Lollis had known Anita personally for a couple of years, and in the months before her murder, he had gone out for drinks or dinner with her quite regularly. He was not aware of Anita's having any other close male companions. Detectives were able to determine that Lollis was the first man Elenes Feliciano (the Conner Hotel resident who'd been in the bar twice the night Anita was killed) had seen in the bar on the night of the crime.

Robert Silva, owner of the Square Rigger Restaurant and Bar (no relation to Joseph Silva), was also interviewed. He was in Fagiani's at about 5:00 p.m. on the night of the murder and stayed for approximately thirty minutes. Silva told investigators the only persons present at the time were Anita, who was tending bar, and an old Italian man, Frank Banchero.

Detectives checked with neighboring businesses on Main Street and the surrounding areas. Lee Soon, owner of the Asia Café next door to Fagiani's, reported something interesting. Soon said his café was closed on Wednesday nights, including the night of Anita's murder. Nevertheless, Soon visited his café at 11:30 p.m. that night to do some work in the kitchen, and he noticed that the Fagiani's sign was on. He thought that was unusual. Even more unusual was the fact that when he left his café at 2:30 a.m. on July 11, the Fagiani's sign was still on. However, Anita's Cadillac was not there.

Shrewd detectives often attend the funerals or memorial services for murder victims because it is not unusual for killers to go to the funerals of their victims. Their behavior mimics that of arsonists, who mingle with the crowd at buildings they have torched; it provides an extra thrill for them as they gloat in their belief that they have fooled everyone. Moreover, murderers who are close to the deceased sometimes feel they risk waving a red flag if they stay away from services.

On July 14, District Attorney James D. Boitano attended the rosary service for Anita Andrews, both as a friend of the Fagiani family and as Napa's chief law enforcement officer. Boitano kept his eyes open for anything or anyone that seemed unusual, and he later reported observing nothing out of the ordinary.

The funeral was held on July 15 at Claffey and Rota Funeral Home, several blocks up Main Street from Fagiani's bar. Two police officers attended. One sat in his car, parked across the street from the funeral home, observing people and vehicles and jotting down license plate numbers. The other officer attended the service to watch for anything or anyone who seemed out of the ordinary. Neither officer observed anything unusual.

In high-profile cases, it is common for people to contact the police with tips. Elwood Cassidy of Napa called in to the police station to say that he had occasionally seen Anita in the Green Door bar with a five-foot, eleven-inch, two-hundred-pound man known to be retired from Mare Island and living in Vallejo. Cassidy described this man as a "known crazy SOB."

In another potential lead, police dispatcher Karen Blakesley told investigators about information provided to her by two of her female friends. On

James D. Boitano, Napa County district attorney and friend of Anita Andrews and her family. *Courtesy of the Napa County Historical Society.*

July 18, eight days after the murder, they were in the Stagecoach Room of the Travelers Pancake House on Soscol Avenue. A Caucasian adult male approached their table. He was approximately fifty years old, five feet, nine inches tall and weighed around 150 pounds. He was gray-haired, very tan, thin-lipped and had a gold crown in the lower left side of his mouth. He was wearing a light blue shirt and light pants. The women said the man told them he was a federal employee, an on-site inspector for the IRS, who collected some kind of license fees. He went on to say he was in Fagiani's bar the night Anita Andrews was killed. He said a man had come in that evening who sat at one end of the bar and waited for Anita to close, then pushed and dragged Anita into the back room, where he beat and raped her. The ostensible IRS inspector also appeared to have a good working knowledge of the Napa State Hospital's alcoholic recovery program. He also stated that money was taken from Anita's wallet rather than from the till.

Based on this alarming information, the police contacted Phillip L. Manfredi, manager of the Stagecoach Room. Manfredi recognized the man from the description and said he was someone he had seen when he worked at the Whistle Stop bar in Yountville. He thought his first name

Obituaries

Anita Andrews

Anita Fagiani Andrews, 51, of 2819 Soscol Ave., No. 14, died Wednesday.

A native of Oakville, born on Aug. 10, 1922, she worked as a secretary at Napa State Hospital for the past 15 years. She was a member of the Sons of Italy, St. Helena, the Pochahantas, the California State Employes Association and St. John's Catholic Church.

Mrs. Andrews is survived by her mother, Mrs. Annie Fagiani of Napa; two daughters, Mrs. Dianne Lee Brown of Maryland, Mrs. Donna Brumfield of Walnut Creek and a sister, Muriel Fagiani of Napa; three uncles, an aunt and a grandchild.

Friends are invited to meet at the Claffey and Rota Funeral Home at 9:15 Monday, thence to St. John's Catholic Church for a Funeral Mass of Christian burial commencing at 9:30 a.m. The Rosary will be recited at 8 p.m. Sunday at the Chapel. Interment will be at Holy Cross Cemetery, St. Helena.

when their motor ya down in heavy seas.

His sister, Mrs. Peters of St. Hele Caspers often travel Napa Valley to visit fi attend wine and food so tions. He was well i many of the county' ment officials.

As a supervisor, specialized in environn fiscal management mi was a leader in the dev of drug abuse and p programs in Orange Cc

The memorial servi held at St. Michael Angels Church, 323. View Drive, Corona de family requests that flowers, donations in n be sent to the Harbor D 3443 Pacific View Dri del Mar, or the Cate Sc Box 68, Carpinteria.

Seymour Schw

Seymour L. Schweit: the late Alvin ar Schweitzer of Napa, d

Left: *Napa Register*, July 12, 1974. Obituary of Anita Andrews. *Napa County Newspaper Archive.*

Below: The gravestone of Anita Andrews. *Courtesy of the Napa County District Attorney's Office.*

was Carl, that he was either a CPA or an accountant and he worked for the federal government.

Following up on this lead, the police contacted Bert Harris, daytime bartender at the Whistle Stop bar in Yountville. Unfortunately, Harris had been employed there only a short time and was unable to provide any useful information. Instead, Harris referred them to the nighttime bartender, Larry True. Eventually, police did contact Larry True, but he was of no help in identifying a viable suspect.

The police followed up on these and many other leads. The vast majority of these were fruitless. However, all leads were thoroughly investigated before they were eventually ruled out. The Napa Police Department did everything possible to solve the case, interviewing numerous witnesses and even contacting other police jurisdictions. Everything turned up negative, but it was not for lack of effort by law enforcement. They never gave up.

7

THE VICTIM'S TAN 1967 CADILLAC

One of the most puzzling questions associated with this murder was what had happened to the victim's tan 1967 Cadillac?

At first there were no leads on its whereabouts. As news of the missing car spread, people began contacting the police. Harvey Anderson, owner of the Mobil gas station on Third Street, was one of those callers. He was unable to provide any insight into the car's location, but he did give the police information that might assist them when they *did* find the car. In the latter part of 1973, Anderson had put a set of new tires on Anita's car with the identifiable brand of Carnegie Classics. The police tucked this information away in their files to aid in identifying the vehicle when they recovered it, which they fully expected to do at some point in the investigation.

Local law enforcement, especially the officers who patrolled Fagiani's bar, were familiar with the victim's automobile and had included a detailed description in their APB. The *Napa Register* also published a description of the vehicle, and out-of-county law enforcement agencies were asked to be on the lookout for that particular car.

On July 19, one Irene Clifton called to say she had seen a four-door tan Cadillac with the first two letters of the license plate UG on Highway 280 between Highway 17 and Foothill Boulevard in Santa Clara County, some seventy miles south of Napa. Napa police forwarded this information to the California Highway Patrol, but they were unable to locate the automobile.

Another significant lead regarding the car, and possibly the murder itself, developed when police received a call on August 9 from Norman Sullivan,

Image of a 1967 Cadillac, the same make and model as Anita Andrews's car. *Courtesy of the Napa County District Attorney's Office.*

special investigator for the Bank of America credit card center in San Francisco. Sullivan stated that he had received an invoice indicating that on July 11, the day after the murder, Anita Andrews's BankAmericard had been used to purchase ten dollars' worth of regular gasoline at V.E. Cristoni's Phillips 66 truck stop, located at 7825 Stockton Boulevard in Sacramento. The license plate number matched that of Anita's Cadillac. The credit card sales slip was signed "A.E. Andrews," and Sullivan forwarded a photostatic copy of the invoice.

Sullivan's report triggered an instantaneous response. The same day, detectives traveled to that Sacramento truck stop and spoke with the assistant manager and other employees. However, no one remembered a purchase associated with the vehicle. Three days later, detectives returned to Sacramento to speak with the employee who had actually served Anita's vehicle on the evening of July 11. Thirty-six-year-old Paul Greiner verified that it was the victim's Cadillac. Greiner stated that the Cadillac driver was at the station on July 11 between 2:00 a.m. and 4:00 a.m., but he did not know from which direction the car had arrived.

He said the driver, the sole occupant of the vehicle, instructed Greiner to fill up the tank and made a ten-dollar gasoline purchase. Greiner described the driver as male, wearing a short-sleeved shirt, but he could not recall the color. The man wore light pants, and the lap area was covered with a white terrycloth towel. Greiner had also noticed that the outer edges of the exposed area below the towel exhibited stains that appeared to be coffee or some other dark-colored liquid.

Greiner estimated that the man was forty to forty-five years of age with darkish-colored hair. His haircut was "standard," with no sideburns.

Cristoni's Truck Stop in Sacramento. The killer presumably stole Anita's Cadillac and stopped here for gas, using her stolen BankAmericard. *Courtesy of the Napa County District Attorney's Office.*

He had a small mouth and thin lips, and his ears were small and flat to the head. He weighed about 175 pounds and was dark-complexioned. Except for the instruction to "fill it up," the driver made no other statement, asked no questions and appeared to be very calm. After the transaction, he left the station, and Greiner did not observe the direction in which the car headed.

This truck stop was located at the junction of Old Highway 99 North and South, approximately four miles from the interstate junctions for Highways 80, 99 and 50 North. There were eight motels around this area, each of which police checked. They learned that on the night of July 11, a man registered at the Park Lane Motel on Stockton Boulevard in Sacramento under the name of C. Van Amber, giving his address as 3179 Linda Vista Avenue in Napa and listing a business affiliation with Napa Drayage & Warehouse Company. No car or truck description appeared on the motel registration form.

The possibility of a Napa-based truck driver spending the night in Sacramento on the evening Anita Andrews's Cadillac was seen at a nearby gas station caught the detectives' attention. But when they followed up, C. Van Amber was ruled out as a possible suspect.

For the first several months after the murder, even when intensive investigation had diminished, the police kept trying to locate Anita's 1967 Cadillac, talking with other law enforcement agencies and blanketing them with "Be on the Lookout" flyers and bulletins. If the car had been acquired and subsequently parted out by an auto dismantler, state agencies require the proprietor to submit paperwork such as a bill of sale showing that the vehicle had been legally acquired and was then legally junked out or sold for parts. The police contacted the appropriate state agencies to see if paperwork regarding the subject vehicle had been submitted. No information on the car was ever found.

The conclusion was obvious. If the car had been junked out, it must have been done improperly, without the appropriate state paperwork. This suggested that another person had helped the perpetrator illegally dispose of the 1967 Cadillac, which presented a daunting task for the police: the suspect could have junked out the car in another state with different regulations than California. Or perhaps he had dismantled it himself.

Despite the hundreds of hours of investigative work devoted to the conscientious work of law enforcement in their search, Anita Andrews's 1967 tan Cadillac, California license plate number UGA370, was never seen or heard of again.

8

PROBLEMS

S olving a homicide is never simple. Sometimes it seems impossible. Most veteran detectives will tell you there is no such thing as an easy murder case. Even in homicides that look as if there will be an expedient solution, twists can occur.

In the case of Anita Andrews's murder, police had very little to go on. They had a missing automobile that remained missing; they had traced it to a truck stop in Sacramento County, but then it seemed to vanish. They also had a copy of the credit card transaction the suspect had used to buy gas, but they were unable to connect it with anyone. They had a description of the driver but could not locate him.

Fingerprints had been collected, but at that time, expertise in fingerprint identification was still developing. It wasn't until 1999 that the Automated Fingerprint Identification System was established; in 1974, police couldn't just enter a fingerprint card into a database and have a match pop up. Also, forensic utilization of DNA data was in the initial stages of development, as were advanced computer capabilities and use of the internet.

What made the Fagiani murder case even more difficult to solve was the fact that it did not fit the basic formula homicide detectives rely on: Motive—Opportunity—Means. In the Fagiani case, motive was a mystery, and this had become an almost insurmountable hurdle.

Detectives were reluctantly concluding that the killer and the victim were complete strangers until the moment of the murder. Therefore, if Anita Andrews had not seen her murderer until shortly before her death, the odds of identifying the killer decreased dramatically because all of the possible subjects who knew the victim would be eliminated as suspects. Nevertheless, police continued to thoroughly examine every possible lead, even those offering little hope of developing into anything meaningful.

As time went by, theories about what had happened became more far-reaching and less plausible. Some of these were explored in an article by John Thill titled "Fagiani's," published on the Explore Napa website, in which various theories were proposed. Some theories centered on the notion of an ex-boyfriend who had run off with a traveling carnival. Others proposed that the notorious Zodiac killer from San Francisco might be responsible, especially since one of the Zodiac murders was committed in the Berryessa area of Napa County.

In his *San Francisco Chronicle* article "Napa Bar Is a Reminder of Old Murder," Sam Whiting presented a range of different theories from law enforcement and family members. District Attorney James D. Boitano developed two theories. One was that something had happened to the killer himself. "But," he allowed, "it couldn't have been an auto accident because we'd have the car. However, that car might be at the bottom of the Sacramento River, along with the killer's body and Anita's credit card." However, given the droughts since 1974, the vehicle or a body probably would have been exposed or would have risen from the river bottom.

Boitano's second theory was that the murder was a setup of some kind. "The car was deliberately driven to Sacramento to mislead the police, make it seem like an isolated drifter incident. That means the killer is alive and out there, and there's got to be some tie to Napa through the Napa State Hospital."

Lieutenant John Bailey, the first investigator on the case, shared Boitano's suspicions. "It always kind of ate at me," Bailey said. "The guy could have bought gas with cash. There was enough money in Anita's purse." Bailey left the Napa police force a year after the murder and later served ten years as the Tiburon police chief. But at the time, he speculated that after leaving a paper trail in Sacramento and heading toward Los Angeles, the murderer had doubled back to the Napa area and was still there, though the car had probably been dismantled.

Lieutenant Robert Jarecki stuck to the random crime theory, though he did admit there were holes in that theory: "Every indication is that it was a transient situation, though it is unclear how the person who took Anita's car keys knew which vehicle was hers."

None of these theories directly addressed the many open questions in the investigation: How did the killer get to the bar? If he was a stranger, how did he happen to be talking with Anita and hanging around when she took cash upstairs? Had the neon sign been left on all night? If so, why didn't someone report it?

Whiting reported that all this time Anita's sister, Muriel Fagiani, kept after the police, and when she didn't, Fagiani's bar itself was there as a reminder. Through the years, Muriel continued to search for her sister's car, explaining that she would continue her search, saying, "Always…Always."

9

THE CASE GOES COLD

Despite their best efforts, investigators were no closer to locating the killer. And unless they got a break in the case, it appeared it would remain that way.

Time passed, new crimes occurred and the police had other cases to investigate. Cold cases with no new leads take a backseat to current cases with fresh leads, and this is what happened to the Anita Andrews murder case. No new leads were uncovered. No additional suspects were identified. There was no one left to question. And there was nowhere else to search.

According to witnesses, Anita had not mentioned being afraid of anyone, though she had verbal arguments with her former boyfriend about his running up a $400 phone bill, and she had kept his tools, which he needed for his job, as collateral for the debt. Still, she had never expressed fear of him. While she may have had disagreements with her ex-husband, there was nothing to indicate they had engendered fear of him. The police department's thorough questioning of Anita's friends and family failed to turn up any suspects other than her boyfriend and her ex-husband. Over time, both were ruled out as suspects.

Unable to develop a motive for the murder, the police gradually concluded that a stranger had seen her in the bar and his interest had led to sexual assault. Anita had been killed where she worked, and while someone had rifled through the contents of her purse, robbery had apparently not been the motive. However, the murder scene was very bloody, and there were signs of a real struggle in the bar. She had obviously fought with her assailant.

In large cities, police departments have many unsolved cases. But in small towns like Napa, very few cases go unsolved. This made the Fagiani murder a source of deep frustration to the District Attorney's Office, starting with James D. Boitano, the district attorney at the time of the murder, and continuing with subsequent district attorneys over the next thirty-seven years. Boitano had been a friend of the victim and her family. He said he thought about the case almost every day when he went to his office, which was around the corner from Fagiani's bar. Even after his retirement, that unsolved murder bothered him more than any other case in his career.

It was equally frustrating for the Napa Police Department. Officer Joe Moore, the first officer on the murder scene, felt the frustration, as did Captain Dewey Burnsed, Lieutenant John Bailey and Sergeant Don Kemper, all of whom were involved with the intense investigation undertaken immediately after discovery of Anita Andrews's body.

For these investigators, it was not only the many hours put in striving to find a killer but also the very real possibility he would kill again.

Cases that remain unsolved for years are known as cold cases, indicating that law enforcement has followed every possible avenue of investigation with no result. The Napa Police Department was no exception. As Napa rolled into a new century, the brutal murder of Anita Andrews had indeed gone cold.

Police departments require sufficient funds and manpower to devote to decades-old cases where no new leads have been uncovered for over thirty years. Such cases are among the most difficult to solve. Witnesses gradually die or disappear. Even the perpetrator of a crime might be deceased. Files and evidence that have been in storage for years could be lost or misplaced. And, as in the case of the Anita Andrews murder, some of the original investigators might no longer be available.

Additionally, public pressure sometimes keeps police departments from devoting time to cold cases because current crimes hold the attention of the press and the public, which want these solved for their own safety. This means there's often little demand for allocation of resources for decades-old cases.

However, cold cases still cry out for justice, and many large police departments are able to devote full-time attention to unsolved cases by establishing what is termed a cold case unit, in which a number of detectives are assigned to concentrate exclusively on old, unsolved crimes. Unfortunately, the Napa Police Department did not have a cold case unit.

10

SCIENTIFIC ADVANCES

T he 1970s, '80s and '90s passed with the police no closer to solving the Anita Andrews murder case, and while occasional newspaper articles dealt with the unsolved crime, they only added to the frustration of the police. Even for the many officers hired since 1974, notoriety surrounding the unsolved murder bolstered their determination to continue the investigation.

Hope never died for Anita's sister, Muriel Fagiani, who was unfailingly dedicated to finding her sister's killer. When Anita died, so did Fagiani's Cocktail Lounge, as Muriel never again opened the bar. She continued to visit the police department, checking its progress and reporting possible new leads she had come up with. Officers have admitted that Muriel's drive to discover the perpetrator and his motive was a significant factor spurring them to keep the case active.

Over the ensuing decades, forensic science grew by leaps and bounds as more sophisticated techniques—techniques that could not have been imagined in 1974—were developed. Among these advances, the computer was a big boon to the scientific community, the legal community and the law enforcement community. Police could now computerize fingerprint systems, and a fingerprint could be circulated among widespread law enforcement agencies within minutes instead of the days or weeks it formerly took.

Over the years, the Napa Police Department continued to test new scientific advances by submitting evidence from the old case to new, developing databases. In August 1984, police sergeants Mike Roth and Jim York sent fifteen latent fingerprints recovered from beer bottles and a Brugal Rum bottle from Fagiani's bar to the California Department of Justice Bureau of Forensic Services–Latent Print program (ALPS). No matches were detected.

A few years later, Sergeant Roth and Officer Patrick McGreal sent twenty-nine latent prints to the same office. No matches were detected.

In 1990, Napa Police Department evidence technician Janet Lipsey reviewed those prints and determined that only those from a few beer bottles were sufficiently detailed for the ALPS program. Those were later resubmitted. Again, no matches were detected.

In 1999, Lipsey noted that prints that had been submitted to ALPS in 1985 and 1989 would be continually checked against incoming prints. Because sophisticated fingerprint identification systems were still developing, those systems were only for the state of California. However, the Department of Justice informed Lipsey that the prints would also be run through the Western Identification Network (WIN).

Again, no matches were found.

In more than a century of crime fighting, DNA analysis has had the biggest impact, and it would revolutionize homicide investigation. Stanford University genetic scientist Kristen Wells gives a succinct review of forty years of DNA history with regard to criminal investigation:

> DNA (deoxyribonucleic acid, a molecule that contains the instructions an organism needs to develop, live, and reproduce) holds the set of instructions necessary to build a human being. This means that, just as you are unique from all other individuals on the planet, your DNA is also unique (unless you have an identical twin).
>
> Forensic scientists rely on DNA's being unique to the individual to solve crimes. Despite the power of DNA in solving crimes, it has only recently played a role. The first conviction using DNA as evidence was that of Tommie Lee Andrews in 1987. Before this time, law enforcement didn't have the tools available to collect and compare different DNA samples. Even in the late 1980s, when DNA was being used in criminal investigations, only certain crimes could benefit from the technology. In the early days of DNA profiling, a large amount of a well-preserved starting sample was required in order to analyze the DNA.
>
> By 1989, these problems were overcome using a technique that could copy and amplify the starting-sample DNA. In addition to being able to work with smaller amounts of sample, the sensitivity of DNA profiling has improved since the mid-1980s.

In the early days of DNA profiling, scientists focused on a few regions of the human genome. Increased knowledge of the human genome has provided scientists with more sections of DNA to use in order to distinguish between individuals. Additionally, the cost of sequencing DNA has made huge strides. In 2001, it cost $100 million to sequence the human genome. Today (2020) that cost has dropped to below $1,000 and continues to fall. As we can affordably sequence DNA, we are able to more definitively distinguish between two even closely related individuals.

In the past forty years, our understanding of DNA has made enormous strides, and as our knowledge increases, DNA becomes a more powerful part of forensic analysis.

With the knowledge that a DNA profile can be detected in body fluids, bones and hair roots using a relatively inexpensive process, this scientific breakthrough has become an incredibly powerful tool in solving crimes. While sophisticated DNA profiling did not exist in 1974, such profiling did exist in the first decade of the twenty-first century.

11

DETECTIVE DON WINEGAR TAKES ON
THE ANITA ANDREWS MURDER

In May 2006, Detective Don Winegar was assigned to the 1974 cold case homicide of Anita Andrews, giving the police renewed hopes of solving the murder.

Winegar attended the University of Nevada–Reno, majoring in criminal justice, and he had past experience as a correctional officer with the Department of Corrections in Napa, where he displayed an aptitude for conflict resolution with the meanest, loudest, most antisocial individuals booked into custody. As a detective, he often would say to a suspect in his genial, empathetic style, "You're not a bad person. You just did a bad thing." It was a highly effective interrogation technique. People, including suspects, tended to like him and, more importantly, to trust him.

In December 1984, when Winegar was first hired as a deputy with the Napa County sheriff-coroner, he had never ridden in a police car, fired a gun or seen a dead body. His boss, Sheriff's Deputy Tom Gorman, let Winegar ride along on some patrol shifts to observe police contacts, law enforcement investigations, use-of-force arrests and bookings at the Napa County Department of Corrections. He later attended Basic Police Officer Service Training, graduating near the top of his class.

As a new deputy sheriff, in addition to coroner duties and evidence collection, Don also began to gain experience in homicide investigations. As part of his initial training, he was driven on patrol. He remembered his field training officer pointing out Fagiani's Cocktail Lounge at 813 Main Street and telling him that the owner, Anita Andrews, had been murdered in 1974 and the homicide had never been solved. He also remembered being told that after the murder, Anita's sister, Muriel Fagiani, had closed the bar down and never reopened it.

That was Winegar's one-minute history lesson about the Anita Andrews murder case.

In 1987, the City of Napa Police Department hired Winegar and assigned him to the Special Weapons and Tactics Team. Later, he was selected to be a hostage negotiator. In 1997, he was assigned to the Investigations Division, where he met veteran investigator Detective Dan Lonergan, one of the finest detectives in the department.

Napa police detective Don Winegar. *Courtesy of Don Winegar.*

Over the course of his career, Winegar received over one thousand hours of advanced Police Officer Service Training. By 1998, he was investigating all homicides in Napa County, working alongside senior officers Ed Knutsen and Dan Lonergan and honing his investigative and interrogation skills in several high-profile homicide cases.

The Napa Police Department Investigations Division required an officer to transfer out of Investigations after four years of service for cross-training in other aspects of the force. In 2001, Winegar returned to the Napa Patrol Division as a corporal. In 2005, he returned to the Investigations Division as a detective. By the time he was assigned the Anita Andrews cold case homicide, Winegar was a skilled investigator and interrogator, having investigated approximately fifty homicides, including coroner investigations, suicides and vehicular homicides.

Winegar was ready to investigate the Fagiani cold case murder.

12

DON WINEGAR BEGINS INVESTIGATION OF THE MURDER

O ver the years, Fagiani's Cocktail Lounge had remained untouched from the moment of the murder, frozen in time. It was surrounded by flourishing new businesses, yet the lounge itself remained empty and rundown. The building stood as an eerie museum, with residents and tourists peering through the windows as they walked by. Every now and then, *Napa Valley Register* reporter Jay Goetting would write about the unsolved Andrews homicide. Because of the notoriety of the case and the continued pressure exerted on the police by Muriel Fagiani, detectives planned to review the case, but because neither the Napa Police Department nor the Sheriff's Office had dedicated cold case homicide units, current investigation work took priority.

In May 2006, Don Winegar was instructed to review the Anita Andrews murder investigation. He was to carry out this assignment while also working on his regular case load of current crimes. Winegar was given two boxes of evidence and the case material (police reports and other paperwork) from the murder investigation.

The original Anita Andrews homicide investigators, Detectives John Bailey and Robert Jarecki, had investigated the case until their respective retirements, and in reviewing the extensive case materials, Winegar was impressed with the dedication and devotion to the case shown by these and other earlier police officers. He also noted that in 2001, highly regarded homicide detective Ed Knutsen had begun to review the case but had been unable to complete his work because of his current homicide caseload.

In his review, Winegar noted that Detective Pete Jerich had remained dedicated to solving the Fagiani murder, and in order to get evidence analyzed by the Department of Justice (DOJ), he became quite inventive. At that time (2001), while DNA analysis was available to police departments, the testing process was expensive. The Napa Police Department lacked sufficient funds to pay for it. Jerich mentioned the Andrews murder case when he attended a Department of Justice DNA class. The DOJ criminalist teaching the class suggested that Jerich send some pieces of evidence to the department for DNA analysis, which he happily did. However, several years passed, and Jerich was transferred out of Investigations before he heard back on the evidence submissions. Winegar noted that either no analysis results had ever been received from the DOJ or those results were missing.

Winegar devoted time to the Anita Andrews murder investigation when his regular caseload permitted. He read through all the homicide investigation records and reviewed all of the photographic evidence. He painstakingly inventoried items in the two boxes of materials and booked them back into evidence in an organized manner.

He also located documentation of the items of evidence collected by Jerich and submitted to the DOJ for analysis in December 2001. Those items included a bar towel collected by criminalist Peter D. Barnett and hair and fingernail scrapings recovered from the victim. However, Winegar could not locate a completed DOJ physical evidence examination report concerning these items.

It is possible the DOJ analysis report had been misplaced in the police department's old case files or the evidence had never been analyzed by the DOJ, even though five years had passed. So, in May 2006, Winegar telephoned the DOJ Crime Lab in Sacramento and spoke with a criminalist, who confirmed they did have possession of evidence submitted by Detective Jerich in December 2001. The criminalist advised Winegar that the evidence had not been analyzed, explaining that with DNA analysis there is a backlog. With a "no suspect" case, the wait is longer.

Winegar responded that the DOJ had been in possession of the submitted evidence since 2001. The criminalist stated that the person assigned to the case was senior criminalist Michelle Terra, who was on maternity leave.

In July 2006, Detective Winegar contacted Criminalist Terra, who confirmed that the DOJ had custody of the evidence received from Detective Jerich in 2001, namely (1) a bar towel found under the Fagiani's bar sink and (2) hair and fingernail scrapings recovered from the victim. Terra confirmed that she had in fact reviewed the evidence and would soon submit her report. She said the bar towel had been analyzed and the victim's blood was found. She said she would send the bar towel to a private laboratory for further testing. Terra indicated that the DOJ did *not* have a photograph of the murder weapon (a screwdriver).

Following the call, Winegar asked his property clerk to search for a photograph of the murder weapon, but the clerk could not locate one.

In August 2006, Winegar received Criminalist Terra's six-page report on the examination of the physical evidence Detective Jerich had submitted in 2001. No male DNA was detected. In November, Winegar received a follow-up report from Terra indicating that the bar towel had been sent to the Serological Research Institute in Richmond, California. In April 2007, he received the Serological Research Institute's report. Senior forensic serologist Gary Harmor concluded that the genetic marker result from the DNA on the bar towel was weak and incomplete. It did reflect a mixture of the victim's blood (DNA) and also that of an unknown male. Importantly, the results were sufficient to exclude Liston Beal, the man who had been in town visiting his ex-wife and daughter and who had been the prime suspect of some of the original investigators.

Detective Winegar had made definite progress, but the partial DNA profile was not enough to solve the murder. It could be compared with known DNA samples, but the police had no DNA from known suspects (other than Liston Beal) to use for comparison. Also, while the DNA files of the Federal Bureau of Investigation were available to any law enforcement agency investigating criminal activity or missing persons, the DNA evidence from the Fagiani murder could not be submitted to the combined DNA index system because the sample profile was not complete. Therefore, police were not able to compare that DNA evidence to all samples contained in the national index system.

This was a disappointment to Winegar in his effort to solve the murder, but it was readily apparent that he had made a good start.

13

WE HAVE A SUSPECT

Don Winegar was encouraged, but he still had a current caseload taking up most of his attention. Nevertheless, he carefully planned further actions to take on the Andrews murder as time permitted. These tasks included:

1. Locating the murder weapon (screwdriver) for forensic analysis
2. Submitting blood smear samples found on the floor leading from the bar to the stairway to forensic analysis
3. Submitting hair found near the northwest corner of the bar for forensic analysis
4. Submitting crushed glass found in the street in front of the bar for fingerprint analysis

Winegar took a significant step forward when he obtained the evidence on his to-do list from the Napa Police Department property room, including the cigarette butt and ashes from an ashtray found on the bar. In November 2007, Winegar submitted these items to the Department of Justice in Sacramento. Michelle Terra was assigned to perform the DNA analysis.

On September 30, 2009, Winegar received Terra's physical examination report, which indicated an unknown male DNA profile had been obtained from the cigarette butt and would be entered into the combined DNA index system (CODIS). For the first time, there was at least a chance they would get a hit.

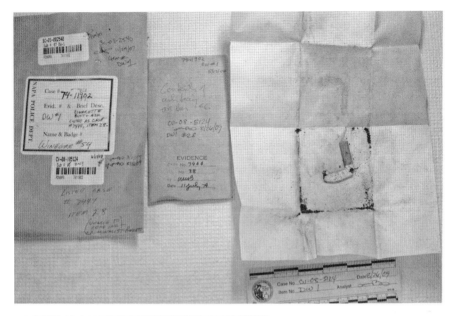

Above: Evidence photo of the cigarette butt and ashes found on the bar after the murder. *Courtesy of the Napa County District Attorney's Office.*

Left: Close-up evidence photo of the cigarette butt and ashes found on the bar after the murder. *Courtesy of the Napa County District Attorney's Office.*

A little over a month later, on November 5, 2009, Winegar was sitting at his desk working on one of his current cases when Terra telephoned. He heard the excitement in her voice and immediately sensed good news. Terra told him that on that very day a CODIS DNA search had been conducted comparing his submitted sample to those in the National DNA Index System (NDIS), and a match had been found. The "candidate match" was identified as Roy A. Melanson, a Colorado State Department of Corrections inmate who was currently incarcerated at Fort Lyon Correctional Facility. Terra also informed Winegar that she had requested a new reference DNA sample from Roy Melanson for comparison and confirmation.

That same day, Terra spoke with Mary Lawrence, supervisor for the Colorado State Department of Corrections Sex Offender Registration and DNA Supervision, who confirmed that Roy Melanson was currently incarcerated for the crime of murder. Lawrence faxed Melanson's offender profile to Terra, who then faxed it to Winegar on November 6, 2009.

As soon as he received the Melanson offender profile fax, he telephoned Mary Lawrence, who confirmed what she had communicated to Terra. When he hung up, Winegar sat back in his chair and tried to restrain himself from being too optimistic. There was now a suspect. He may have been discovered thirty-five years after Anita Andrews was murdered, but the police now had a suspect. However, he knew it was premature to celebrate. It was time to make another list of things to do.

Some obvious tasks came to mind. First, he would bring the Napa County district attorney in on the case. Then he would request a search warrant for evidence from suspect Roy Melanson. Winegar wanted to personally interview Melanson. No one knew the case better than he did, and he wanted answers. Who was Melanson? Why had he been in Napa? Had he known Anita Andrews before July 10, 1974? And if he had committed this murder, why did he do it?

14

A TRIAL TEAM IS FORMED

Winegar's first move was to look into the circumstances of the conviction that had led to Roy Melanson's being housed at Fort Lyon Correctional Facility in Colorado. He discovered that on October 1, 1993, Melanson had been convicted of the first-degree murder of Michele C. Wallace in Gunnison County, Colorado, which had occurred sometime between August 29 and September 1, 1974. He was serving a life sentence.

This fact hit Winegar right between the eyes. The murder of Anita Andrews occurred in Napa sometime between 10:00 p.m. on July 10, 1974, and 9:00 a.m. on July 11, 1974. Approximately fifty days later, Melanson had murdered Michele Wallace in Colorado. That was shocking in and of itself. If Melanson had murdered Anita Andrews, then he was a serial killer.

Winegar went to see District Attorney Gary Lieberstein, a veteran criminal prosecutor serving his third term in office. Lieberstein reviewed the case and assigned it to Deputy District Attorney Paul Gero. Winegar brought the DNA results to Gero, who began to develop a plan for prosecuting the legal case.

Within a few days, Gero invited Winegar to be part of his prosecution team. Winegar had worked several child abuse and sexual assault cases with Gero, and Winegar liked and respected him. Not all district attorney trial deputies treated the police as team members, nor did they work closely with them on a trial. In fact, it was not uncommon for an investigating officer to show up in court, police report in hand, and be put on the stand with no witness preparation. Gero, however, treated police officers with respect, valuing their input in the process.

Gero also requested that district attorney investigator Leslie Severe be assigned to the case. Severe had been an investigator with the Napa District Attorney's Office for approximately nine years. She had considerable formal training and practical experience.

District attorney investigators are law enforcement officers, but instead of working for the police department or the sheriff's office, they work directly with the District Attorney's Office. Winegar did not know Investigator Severe very well, but they had worked together on a few of Gero's prosecutions. Nevertheless, Gero, Severe and Winegar quickly coalesced into a team because they shared one goal: to bring justice on behalf of Anita Andrews, her family and the Napa community.

Gero divided up the work. He would research the legal documents (prior arrests and convictions Melanson may have had) to see if they could be used in trial. Severe would track down persons to be interviewed, and Winegar would be in charge of marshaling Napa Police Department information on the case.

Gero wanted to obtain a search warrant so his team could visit Melanson in prison to interview him and secure his fingerprints, a handwriting sample and DNA material. Judge Steven Kroyer signed the Napa County Superior Court search warrant authored by Winegar.

Winegar was excited about the interview at Fort Lyon Correctional Facility. Together with Sergeant Tim Cantillon and Deputy District Attorney Paul Gero, he flew to Colorado, rented a car and drove to the prison. He knew he could not force Melanson to talk to him, and he and Gero discussed Miranda warning issues. Miranda warnings, the well-known verbal warnings of a suspect's right to remain silent and right to an attorney (free if he couldn't afford one) and that anything said in an interview could be used against him in a court of law, are necessary when a person is in police custody and not free to leave. In a custodial situation, Winegar would be required to read Melanson his Miranda rights. However, Gero and Winegar believed a Miranda warning would not be required as long as Melanson did not feel he was being detained and was free to leave at any time.

When Gero, Cantillon and Winegar drove up to the facility in Colorado, they were surprised to see that it did not look like a high-security prison. The brick buildings were surrounded by barbed wire fencing and a security gate, but some inmates were roaming around and sitting on benches. There seemed to be few guards. Winegar, noticing the grassy landscape

Detective Don Winegar, Napa District Attorney's Office investigator Leslie Severe and Deputy District Attorney Paul Gero in the Fagiani's building in 2011. *Courtesy of the Napa County District Attorney's Office.*

and the "campus" feel, couldn't help thinking that Melanson—a convicted murderer—might have manipulated the system to avoid being housed in a tough high-security prison.

Armed with the search warrant, Winegar, Cantillon and Gero met with Department of Corrections criminal investigator Gregory Kirkland, who had been Winegar's original contact and had assisted him in obtaining the search warrant. Kirkland led the three men to a second-floor room where the interview would take place. It was approximately ten feet by thirty feet with a wooden door on each side, both of which were unlocked and would remain unlocked during the meeting. Winegar remembered thinking that the walls looked like hospital walls. The room had a hidden VCR camera to record the interview, which connected to an adjoining room where Gero and Cantillon would watch on a television monitor and could communicate with Winegar by texting on their cellphones.

Winegar later mentioned that Gero and Cantillon did in fact text him with questions during the interview, and he admitted he felt somewhat inhibited knowing his sergeant and the prosecutor were watching him work and suggesting questions he should be asking. However, he understood Gero and Cantillon needed to be sure he asked all the questions necessary to elicit answers to corroborate charges that might be filed against Melanson.

Before Melanson's arrival, Gero decided that Melanson should sit at a four-foot circular table placed near the door, with nothing blocking the suspect's ability to leave. There were only two chairs at the table. Winegar would sit across from Melanson, whose chair would be next to the unlocked door, so he would be free to leave. Winegar was careful to deny Melanson (or his attorney) any future reason to challenge the legality of the interview.

In setting up the interview room, Winegar noticed that the VCR looked outdated and the TV picture in the adjacent room was not the clearest. Because he had his small digital tape recorder with him, he decided he would also record the interview "just in case." Later, that turned out to be a good move because the VCR tape recording skipped and had poor sound quality. Winegar eventually ended up taking both the VCR tape and the digital recording to an audio studio in Napa, which merged the two.

Because the search warrant allowed Winegar to obtain fingerprints, a writing sample and DNA, he had a nurse standing by to assist. Investigator Kirkland then requested that the suspect come to the interview room. Several minutes went by. Winegar was waiting in the upstairs office with Gero and Cantillon when he looked out the window and saw a man walking unescorted and without cuffs or other restraints across the field area next to the building. As he drew closer, Winegar recognized the man from his mug shots. It was Roy Melanson.

Once Melanson entered the building, he was met by Investigator Kirkland, who escorted him from there. Outside the office, Winegar could hear Kirkland and Melanson approaching. Winegar felt his blood pressure rise. Emotions raced through him as he realized that in just a few moments he would be talking to the person who probably killed Anita Andrews. He was determined to remain calm during the interview and not come on too strong—Melanson might cut it short, as he had every right to do. In fact, Winegar figured it was likely that no matter how cool he was, Melanson, a convicted murderer and lifelong criminal, would not talk to him. But he at least wanted to see the man in person. Up until this moment, he had seen only photographs of him, most of which were thirty-five years old.

Now the time had arrived. In moments, the suspected murderer and the detective would meet in the same room to talk about a crime that had occurred over thirty-five years before.

15

THE INTERVIEW WITH THE SUSPECT

Winegar knew this interview with Roy Melanson would be the most important one in his career. He was determined to control himself and question the suspect in his usual calm manner since he knew maintaining his composure would be crucial. He knew the evidence against Melanson was weak. DNA on a cigarette butt matched Melanson's, but that cigarette butt had been found on top of the bar. No forensic evidence put Melanson in the storage room where Anita Andrews had been murdered. Winegar also knew the prosecution's case could be weakened or lost if he came on too strong and badgered Melanson to the point where he terminated the interview before any important admission or denial could be elicited.

But Don Winegar was a pro's pro. He had invested several years on the Anita Andrews murder case, and he was not going to let himself get rattled. He was not going to change his interrogation style just because this was the most important case of his career. And he wasn't going to choke during the interview just because he was sitting across from the man who might have brutally murdered Anita Andrews.

Winegar was ready.

Accompanied by Investigator Kirkland, Roy Melanson walked into the interview room. When he entered, he looked directly at Winegar. Winegar looked straight back at him.

Melanson was about seventy years old, with a large bald head, broad chest and big stomach. He wore a green prison uniform (similar to medical scrubs but made of heavier fabric) and dark-rimmed glasses. Winegar's observation

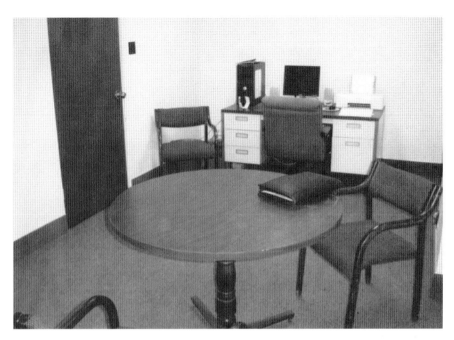

The interview room at Fort Lyon Correctional Facility, Colorado, where Detective Winegar interviewed Roy Melanson. *Courtesy of the Napa County District Attorney's Office.*

Inmate Roy Melanson in the interview room at Fort Lyon Correctional Facility. *Courtesy of the Napa County District Attorney's Office.*

was that Melanson, although recognizable, did not much resemble the thirty-five-year-old photographs Winegar had studied.

Melanson appeared to be healthy and walked with a steady gait (unlike his future court appearances, when he appeared in a wheelchair; Winegar later decided this was an attempt to gain sympathy from the jury).

Winegar introduced himself. Speaking in an even, confident tone, Melanson identified himself to Winegar. They shook hands. Melanson sat down at the interview table near the unlocked door. Winegar decided this was a good sign; Melanson might be more willing to talk to him if he did not feel trapped.

With both the VCR and his small digital recorder turned on, Winegar's plan was to get the interview started, get himself settled and start Melanson talking. He explained that he was a Napa police detective and wanted to talk about something that had occurred there in 1974.

Melanson immediately responded he had never been to Napa. He went on, "Where is that, Napa?"

Winegar replied that Napa was in California. Melanson said, "Okay."

Winegar said he wanted Melanson to know that he was not being detained in the room and he was not in Winegar's custody. He said the door was unlocked. Melanson responded, "Yes, sir. I got nothing to hide."

Melanson went on to volunteer that he had been to California only "one time," in the 1960s. The visit involved himself and some friends who had briefly crossed into Needles from southern Nevada just to say they had been in California. He said he had heard of Napa Valley on television but had never been to the Bay Area or anywhere else in California. "I've never been there."

It was not lost on Winegar that, with Melanson claiming he had never been in Napa, he had already caught the suspect in a lie because his DNA had been found at the crime scene. This fact could be used against him to diminish his credibility. Winegar was careful not to show any elation or emotion.

Still working to create a comfortable momentum to the interview, Winegar asked several questions about Melanson's identity. The suspect explained his full name was Roy Allen Melanson and gave his date of birth as February 13, 1937. He admitted to using other names as aliases.

Careful to use a quiet, conversational tone of voice, Winegar explained that he was investigating a crime that had occurred in Napa in 1974. Melanson responded, "That is when this crime here [his current criminal conviction for murder] was supposed to have happened." Then he explained that in 1974 he was "here in the mountains, working" for a man named Frank Spadafora. Then, beginning around June 1974, he was associated with "the Harvey family," working in the Gunnison Mountains at Crested Butte. He said his work with the Harveys extended through the entire summer of 1974.

Winegar asked Melanson where he had been prior to living in Gunnison County. Melanson answered that he had been living with his father and mother in Orange Field, Texas, for approximately two years. Before that, he had been incarcerated in a Texas prison. He said this part of his life had been investigated as part of the prosecution for the crime for which he was currently incarcerated. He said his time in Orange Field could be verified but did not explain how.

Then Winegar cut to the chase. He explained that he was investigating a murder that had occurred on July 10, 1974, at Fagiani's bar at 813 Main Street in Napa, California, stating, "I'm here investigating to see if possibly you had anything to do with that homicide....What happened is she was brutally stabbed with an object, and I wanted to see if you had anything to do with that."

Melanson responded, "I swear to God I never did. I hate to hear something like that, and I'm very, very serious about that. I was raised different. I know what I'm here for now, but I was raised different than that." He told Winegar he was not an atheist and he believed in God.

At this point, Melanson redirected the conversation, telling Winegar he had gone to Gunnison County in Colorado around June 1974 because he had a friend who lived west of Gunnison, in Montrose, Colorado. He said he did not own an automobile, so he got rides from friends when traveling. When he came to Gunnison County in June or July 1974 he had initially stayed with other friends at their home and then in a trailer with "some Basque people."

Seeing that Melanson was about to continue on what felt like an endless odyssey, Winegar politely interrupted him to explain that he was in Colorado to determine whether Melanson was involved in the crime he was investigating. Melanson responded unequivocally, "No, sir."

Winegar then went on to explain that the murder in Napa had occurred approximately fifty days before the murder for which Melanson had been convicted and was currently serving time.

Melanson responded, "I was right there in Crested Butte."

Winegar turned the interview to the question of whether Melanson smoked. Melanson admitted to smoking cigarettes in the past but said he suffered from emphysema and COPD.

Winegar asked if Melanson had ever been in the military. Melanson said no.

Winegar then told Melanson that crime scene specialists had obtained DNA evidence and fingerprints at the Fagiani murder scene in Napa and advised Melanson that *his* DNA profile had been discovered. Melanson stated, "I'd say it is wrong. It cannot be. It definitely cannot be." He continued, "I couldn't have been in that bar. I was here. How could I be two different places? And I don't even know where Napa Valley is."

Melanson wasn't through. "On my dead mother's grave, I had nothing to do with anything that you have discussed. I am not capable of that, nor was I capable of it even back then." He added that his parents had raised him right. And then, somewhat ambiguously, he went on to say that on a lot of things he "just didn't do right."

Winegar again asked about Melanson's DNA being found at the crime scene.

Melanson answered, "You don't have mine unless they came here and got it." He asserted that DNA can be manipulated, and he knew of an "eastern states" investigation where a woman falsified a DNA profile. He said that, on his current conviction, the police investigation had never discovered a cause of death, and that the television show detailing the Michele Wallace murder investigation was "lying." (Michele Wallace's body was found many years after her death, but the skeletal remains provided no cause of death. Melanson was convicted on other evidence.)

Pulling the interview back to the Napa murder case, Winegar told Melanson that a cause of death *did* in fact exist and again asserted that Melanson's DNA had been found at the crime scene. Melanson retorted, "It ain't mine. I don't care what you got. I wasn't there. I'm telling you I didn't do nothing like that."

Winegar asked if Melanson had stolen Anita Andrews's Cadillac or her purse. Melanson, appearing resistive, denied responsibility, responding several times, "I'd have to have been there, sir."

Winegar pressed on. "Your DNA came up as being there. All the science points to you, and so I need you to explain it in a better way than, 'It wasn't me.'"

Becoming antagonistic, Melanson responded, "Well, okay, then I'll explain it with an attorney. I'm gonna let a lawyer show you. May I have your name and everything on paper?"

Winegar replied, "Oh, I'll give you everything, sir."

Melanson shook his head, "Sir, I swear to God there is something wrong somewhere."

Winegar said, "All right. Thank you," and exited the interview room. He called Kirkland back into the room and asked the nurse to take the blood draw. Fingerprints and a handwriting sample were also taken. Melanson was escorted out of the office by Kirkland and disappeared quickly without a word spoken.

Before the interview, Gero and Winegar had discussed how criminal suspects vary in their responses to interrogation. Some confess. Some make certain admissions. Some lie about just "passing through." And others deny everything. It was apparent to Winegar that Melanson had chosen this last course. Melanson had denied ever being in Napa or in California except for his brief visit to Needles. He had maintained this even when Winegar disclosed that the Napa police identified his DNA at the murder scene. Winegar had further disclosed that the police found Melanson's fingerprints at the crime scene. Even this had not budged Melanson from his denials.

There had been no admission, but Winegar was happy. Melanson had started out in a polite, southern-accented voice. In his laid-back interview style, Winegar had given the impression he believed everything Melanson was saying. He even told him it would be a short interview since Melanson had never been to California.

However, it had turned out to be a long interview. Cantillon and Gero were ecstatic. Winegar had been at his best. His quiet, nonthreatening interrogation had allowed him to have a calm discussion with Melanson and to elicit important information. Ironically, Melanson's style was similar to Winegar's; they each came across as agreeable people and easy conversationalists. The difference was that Winegar was dealing with truth and facts; Melanson was not. He denied involvement in the Anita Andrews murder, as he had also denied his involvement in the Michele Wallace murder in Colorado, even though the evidence overwhelmingly supported his conviction of that crime.

Winegar knew he had gained some important information from the interview. He had caught Melanson in a lie since he had denied ever being in California and specifically in Napa, when the DNA evidence from the cigarette butt proved that Melanson *had* in fact been in Fagiani's bar. Melanson's denial of this fact alone could be enough to destroy his credibility and lead to his conviction.

Winegar also had knowledge of Melanson's conviction in the Michele Wallace murder in Colorado, and this fact could be used against him in a trial. However, while the case against him was growing stronger, it was still somewhat sketchy in terms of proof beyond a reasonable doubt, which is what the prosecution required.

Detective Don Winegar in the interview room at Fort Lyon Correctional Facility. *Courtesy of the Napa County District Attorney's Office.*

After the interview, Winegar rejoined Cantillon and Gero, who were thrilled with the results. Melanson had thought he could manipulate the interview. But Winegar had gotten a convicted murderer in prison to talk to him and to put on the record some easily disproven lies.

The beer tasted good that evening.

16

THE PHOTO LINEUP

B ack at his Napa office, Winegar contacted Mary Lawrence at the Colorado Department of Corrections to request the DNA buccal (mouth) swab evidence and a blood sample from Melanson to go along with fingerprints and a writing sample procured from Melanson during the prison visit.

On December 7, 2009, Winegar sent the DNA buccal swab and blood sample evidence received from Mary Lawrence to the California Department of Justice in Sacramento for classification and comparison with existing evidence from the crime scene. He also asked Napa Police Department forensic evidence specialist Janet Lipsey to compare Melanson's fingerprints to the latent fingerprints recovered from the crime scene. By the end of December, Lipsey confirmed that the crime scene prints were definitely Roy Melanson's. Winegar couldn't help but admire the work of the original police detectives and the original criminalist in charge of the case back in 1974. Preserving that evidence might make it possible, over three decades later, to identify the person responsible for Anita Andrews's murder.

Now Detective Winegar decided to interview witness David Luce, one of three customers in Fagiani's bar on the evening of the murder. Luce had originally been interviewed by Officer Joe Moore and Detective John Bailey on July 11, 1974. He was now living in a care facility in Chico, California, with a diagnosis of terminal cancer. Winegar arranged to drive to Chico to meet with him. His goals for this interview were twofold: to confirm what

Luce had told Moore and Bailey and to show him a photo lineup, hoping for a positive identification of Roy Melanson.

For a photo lineup to be admissible in court, Winegar knew the photos must be as similar as possible; no single photo in the lineup could be suggestive of the suspect. He was determined to make his photo lineup as fair as possible.

To construct his lineup, he began by looking at old 1970s black-and-white booking photographs of Melanson, obtained from the Orange, Texas Sheriff's Department. Winegar had his police evidence technician remove lettering and numbers from a Roy Melanson photo previously sent to him and entered that into the computer system. He also located some old Polaroid booking photos of Napa County individuals but found nothing appropriate.

In composing a photo lineup, the Napa Police Department used a computer system with booking photos of individuals from surrounding counties. Winegar searched this system for photos of men about the same age, height, weight and body type as Melanson. Still worried about the lineup, he recalled he must have bored his co-workers by showing them many possible photo lineups and asking their opinion. Finally, he constructed what he believed to be a fair photo lineup. Because these were color photos, he made them all black-and-white.

In January 2010, Winegar met David Luce at his care facility. Before allowing Luce to view the photos, Winegar read a photo lineup admonition the police use to ensure that the viewer is properly advised:

> *In a moment I'm going to show you a group of photographs. This group of photographs may or may not contain the picture of the person who committed the crime now being investigated. Keep in mind that hair types, beards, and mustaches may easily be changed. Also, photographs may not always depict the true complexion of a person. They may be lighter or darker than is shown in the photograph. Pay no attention to any markings or numbers that may appear on the photos. When you have looked at all the photographs, tell me whether you have seen the person who you think committed the crime. Do not tell any other persons whether you have or have not identified anyone.*

Luce said he understood the admonition and signed an acknowledgment. Then Winegar showed him six photographs. They included one of the suspect, Roy Melanson, taken on April 4, 1975, by the Orange, Texas Sheriff's Department.

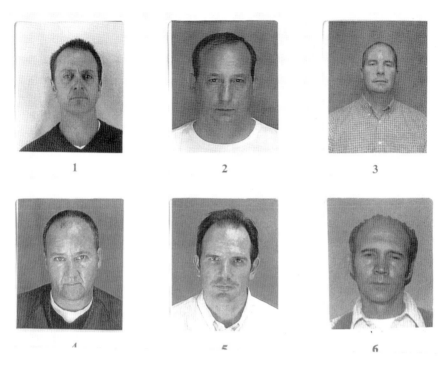

The black-and-white photo lineup constructed by Detective Winegar to show to witness David Luce. *Courtesy of the Napa County District Attorney's Office.*

Luce studied the photo lineup for approximately forty-five seconds. "If I had to pick someone out, I would pick this one." He pointed to photo no. 6. It was the photo of Melanson. Luce said he recognized the eyes. But looking up at Winegar, he added that he was not 100 percent sure, as he had not seen Melanson before or since that evening.

Winegar was gratified when David Luce picked out Melanson's photograph. He was also pleased to confirm that Luce's current statements to him during the interview were consistent with his original statements to Napa police detectives. Winegar, of course, was thoroughly familiar with the police report, but hearing the recollections directly from Luce himself was deeply satisfying.

Things were coming together. With the DNA evidence and Luce as a witness, Winegar knew he could prove beyond a reasonable doubt that Melanson had been in Napa and at Fagiani's bar on the night of the Anita Andrews murder. He hoped David Luce would be alive for the trial, but as Luce stated, "I am already beyond my expiration date." As a precaution,

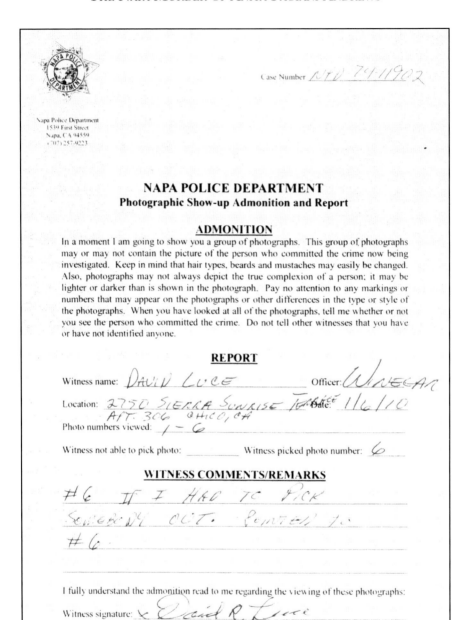

Case Number *NPD 74-11902*

Napa Police Department
1539 First Street
Napa, CA 94559
(707) 257-9223

NAPA POLICE DEPARTMENT
Photographic Show-up Admonition and Report

ADMONITION

In a moment I am going to show you a group of photographs. This group of photographs may or may not contain the picture of the person who committed the crime now being investigated. Keep in mind that hair types, beards and mustaches may easily be changed. Also, photographs may not always depict the true complexion of a person; it may be lighter or darker than is shown in the photograph. Pay no attention to any markings or numbers that may appear on the photographs or other differences in the type or style of the photographs. When you have looked at all of the photographs, tell me whether or not you see the person who committed the crime. Do not tell other witnesses that you have or have not identified anyone.

REPORT

Witness name: *DAVID LUCE*   Officer: *WINEGAR*

Location: *2750 SIERRA SUNRISE TERRACE* Date: *1/6/10*
APT. 306 CHICO, CA
Photo numbers viewed: *1 - 6*

Witness not able to pick photo: _____ Witness picked photo number: *6*

WITNESS COMMENTS/REMARKS

#6 IF I HAD TO PICK
SOMEBODY OUT. POINTED TO
#6.

I fully understand the admonition read to me regarding the viewing of these photographs:

Witness signature: *David R. Luce*

Date: *01/06/10*   Time: *0956 HRS*

"Photographic Show-Up Admonition and Report" signed by David Luce, identifying Roy Melanson as the man he saw in Fagiani's Cocktail Lounge on July 10, 1974. *Courtesy of the Napa County District Attorney's Office.*

Key witness David Luce in his care facility in Chico, California. *Courtesy of the Napa County District Attorney's Office.*

Winegar would soon arrange for Luce's testimony to be recorded in case he died before the trial.

Winegar was also troubled by the fact that approximately fifty days after the murder of Anita Andrews, Melanson had murdered Michele Wallace in Gunnison, Colorado. That meant he needed to track down Melanson's whereabouts during that fifty-day period. Where had he been before his appearance in Napa? And where had he gone following his appearance in Gunnison, Colorado?

17

WHO WAS ROY MELANSON?

Paul Gero wanted Winegar and Leslie Severe to dig into Melanson's past. What made Melanson tick? What was he like? Temperament? Personality? Was he able to get people to trust him or get close to people quickly? Was he married? Did he have children? Who *was* Roy Melanson?

On January 14, 2010, Winegar spoke to one Bonnie Vidrine, who told him that in 1973 she had lived in Hammond, Louisiana, where she had become pregnant by Roy Melanson. In early 1974, Melanson and Vidrine drove to Tucson, Arizona, where they began living in a motel. Vidrine described Melanson as "an intelligent and convincing talker." Not long after their arrival, Vidrine said they had an argument, and Melanson walked out, leaving her without a car. She never saw him again. Vidrine returned to Louisiana. A few months later, on May 15, 1974, their son was born.

Winegar concluded that while Melanson was apparently a persuasive talker, it was apparent he was also a man who felt no responsibility to a woman who was carrying his child. But nothing in Vidrine's comments hinted that Melanson might be a serial killer.

However, it wasn't long before Winegar and Severe began to unearth far more disturbing information about Melanson's past. What the two investigators discovered was a history of rape and murder perpetrated by Roy Melanson, starting with the March 29, 1962 rape of Rhonda T. in Jefferson County, Texas. The young woman was driving home from work when she noticed a vehicle in her rearview mirror, flashing its headlights. Thinking it was the police, she pulled over. It was Roy Melanson. He pulled her out of her car, placed her in his vehicle and drove her somewhere near a bridge, where he raped her. He then drove her back to her vehicle, demanding that she "never tell anyone about what happened." She reported the attack to police. Melanson was convicted of rape on October 11, 1963, and sentenced to twelve years in prison.

After Melanson's attack on Rhonda T., but before his arrest, Melanson attacked and attempted to rape his sixteen-year-old cousin Sandra Chisholm on June 12, 1962, in Pinehurst, Texas. Sandra stated she was asleep when she awoke to find a man on top of her. At ninety-five pounds, she was unable to fight Melanson off. Testifying at the trial, she described him as "a very big strong monster." She begged and screamed for him to leave, threatening that her father was coming home, to which Melanson responded, "No, he's not, I just left him." He ignored her pleas, but the assault was interrupted when automobile headlights flashed through the bedroom window.

Sandra ran outside to a neighbor's house and banged on the door for help. She reported the crime to her father and to the police, and she later testified against Melanson in court. Winegar and Severe were unable to determine from the available records whether the prosecution resulted in a conviction.

Further investigation led to records of another assault after Melanson's release from prison for the Rhonda T. rape conviction. On August 8, 1972, Katherine Ortiz was driving on Highway 87 to Port Arthur, Texas, when a tire blew out. Ten minutes later, Melanson and a young boy in a truck pulled over to aid her. Melanson drove Ortiz to get a spare tire, and on the way back to her car he dropped the boy off and pulled into a clearing off the road. Ortiz demanded, "What the hell are you doing?"

Melanson grabbed her, and Ortiz began to fight for her life. She later said Melanson "went wild," hitting her several times in the mouth with his fist. When she called him "an animal," he threatened that she would get more if she didn't sit still.

He pulled off her chain belt and started to choke her, fell on top of her and told her to keep quiet or it would be worse. He then pulled her slacks and panties completely off her left leg, leaving her right thigh covered. He pulled up her sweater and ripped off her brassiere. He pulled his pants down to his knees and violently raped her, forced her to perform fellatio on him and sodomized her for approximately two hours. Then he drove her to a gas station, fixed her flat tire and let her go.

Katherine drove to her brother's house and called the police. The case later went to trial, and Katherine testified under oath that Melanson had acted "savagely." Winegar and Severe were again unable to determine from the records whether Melanson had been convicted.

As Winegar and Severe would discover, that was just the tip of the iceberg.

On February 20, 1974 (five months before the murder of Anita Andrews), seventeen-year-old Sandra Sue Arnold drove to a gas station near Bridge City, Texas, to get gasoline. She was approached at the station by Melanson, who pretended to need help with his vehicle. He persuaded her to get in his truck, whereupon he grabbed her by the hair, threw her down and threatened to kill her if she moved. Then he drove to a field and raped her.

Sandra said later she thought she would be freed, but Melanson drove to a garbage dump and raped her again; gagged her; bound her hands, arms, feet and legs with pantyhose and rope; and moved her to another car. Threatening to kill her with a gun, he drove across the border to Louisiana and forced her into the woods, where he raped her two or three more times.

Arnold eventually convinced Melanson to let her go by promising she would tell her parents that, instead of being abducted, she had run away from home. He left her on the side of the road. When she was rescued, she reported the kidnapping and rape to the police. In September 1974, Melanson was arrested. He was convicted of aggravated rape, and on November 5, 1975, he was sentenced to life in prison. (Melanson was later released on March 21, 1988.)

After Melanson's rape of Sandra Sue Arnold in February 1974, he made his way to Napa, where he murdered Anita Andrews on July 10. About seven weeks later, on August 30, 1974, twenty-five-year-old Michele Wallace, a landscape photographer from Chicago, was visiting Colorado for a five-day backpacking and photography trip. She offered a ride to two men who were apparently having car trouble outside the small town of Gunnison, Colorado. The two men were Roy Melanson and a casual acquaintance, Charles Matthews. Michele dropped Matthews off at a local bar and drove on with Melanson. On September 3, Michele's mother reported to the police that her daughter was missing. Despite an extensive search, police could find neither Michele nor her car. Later, Melanson was sighted at a friend's house in Gunnison, driving Michele's car. He left Colorado in her car, pawned a backpack and sleeping bag in Kansas and pawned various other items in Iowa. He then abandoned the car in Texas and returned to Pueblo, Colorado, with another acquaintance.

On September 12, 1974, Melanson was arrested on a Texas warrant for the Sandra Sue Arnold attack. When police searched his car, they discovered Michele Wallace's car keys, Bank of America credit card and car insurance

Michele Wallace, murdered by Roy Melanson in 1974, only weeks after he killed Anita Andrews. *Courtesy of the Napa County District Attorney's Office.*

information. Initially, Melanson denied ever driving with Michele or being a passenger in her car, but the following day he told an FBI agent he had gone to a bar with Michele and had stolen her car. At that time, Melanson was not charged with her murder.

In July 1979, a scalp with hair tied in braids, similar to Michele's hairstyle, was found near a creek in Gunnison, Colorado. It wasn't until August 1991 that Investigator Kathy Young of the Gunnison County Sheriff's Department requested the Colorado Bureau of Investigation to compare the discovered scalp and braided hair with hair from a hairbrush belonging to Michele Wallace. The hair samples matched, and in April 1992, Melanson was arrested and charged with first-degree murder. Four months later, a new search uncovered a human skull, some thread, buttons, a zipper, a brassiere and a hiking boot with a skeletal foot inside. A dentist and odontologist confirmed that the teeth and skull belonged to Michele Wallace.

On September 1, 1993, Melanson was found guilty of the first-degree murder of Michele Wallace and was sentenced to life in prison.

Melanson was released from prison on the Sandra Sue Arnold conviction on March 21, 1988. On July 2, 1988, fifty-year-old Pauline Klumpp informed her husband, who was working out of town at Todd's Shipyard in Galveston, Texas, that she was going to stop by their rental house in Port Arthur to retrieve her television set because she feared the renters would move out and steal it. At the time, Melanson was staying in the Klumpps' rental with his ex-wife, Brenda Melanson; her daughter and son; and her boyfriend, Dolph Walker.

Pauline arrived, retrieved her television set and placed it on the front passenger seat of her car. Melanson offered to go with her to check on the air conditioner at her residence in Port Arthur. He got into the backseat, and she drove away.

On July 4, Pauline's husband returned to their home from his out-of-town job to find the door to the house closed but unlocked. Pauline's purse was inside and the clothes in her closet undisturbed. An outside cookstove had been left on, with burned chicken inside, and their dog had been left without food or water. Pauline's car was found at a grocery store with the doors unlocked and the television set on the front seat. Her husband suspected foul play and called police. Police investigators searched for jewelry and a .22-caliber pistol belonging to Pauline but were unable to locate them.

On April 19, 2011, Investigator Leslie Severe interviewed Dolph Walker, the boyfriend of Melanson's ex-wife, in Orange, Texas. Walker told them Melanson occasionally went to Houston to rob people of their jewelry. When he returned with rings, bracelets and necklaces, Walker functioned as the middleman, pawning the jewelry for him in Port Arthur. Walker also remembered Melanson leaving his rented house with Pauline Klumpp and saying, "I'm going to get me some of that." When Walker responded that Pauline was not interested, Melanson replied, "You don't know me, I did it before and I will do it again. One way or the other, I will get it." That conversation took place the day Pauline Klumpp disappeared. Her body was never found.

On August 5, 1988, twenty-four-year-old Charlotte Sauerwin was engaged to be married and living in Livingston Parish, Louisiana. In the late morning, she went to the local Laundromat, where she was seen conversing with a stranger in the area who claimed to be "Cajun." Around 1:00 p.m. or 2:00 p.m. that day, Sauerwin went to a mechanic's shop to pay a bill. She was never seen alive again.

Around 7:00 p.m., Sauerwin's fiancé, John Lejeune, returned home from work and made dinner. By 9:00 p.m., when Charlotte had not shown up, he became concerned, called her parents and friends and drove around searching for her car, which he finally found on a gravel road adjacent to property they owned. By 11:15 p.m. that night, with no sign of Sauerwin, Lejeune called police to report her missing, and the Livingston Parish Sheriff's Department dispatched deputies to search for her.

They found her body approximately three hours later, lying facedown with her legs spread apart and her left arm extended. She had on a shirt and socks but no shoes; her pants and panties had been removed from her left leg and lay over her right leg. Her engagement ring, earrings and purse were missing, as were her handgun and some car audio equipment. Jim Churchman from the Louisiana State Crime Laboratory analyzed the crime scene and collected forensic evidence, including Charlotte's socks, and her body was then moved to a funeral home for an autopsy.

Forensic pathologist Dr. E. Laga determined that the cause of death was strangulation and/or stab wound to the right side of her neck. The missing pistol was a Beretta 380, purchased by Charlotte in 1986. On October 17, 1988, Kentucky State Police detective John Carr seized the weapon after a citizen in East View, Kentucky, reported Roy Melanson had sold it to him four days before. Detective Carr also seized a diamond ring matching the description of Charlotte's engagement ring. Melanson had given the ring to a female friend.

On November 6, 1990, Melanson was convicted of burglary, possession of a handgun by a convicted felon and receiving stolen property. He was sentenced to two years in Kentucky State Prison.

In 2010, Kentucky authorities finally conducted DNA testing on seminal fluid found on one of Sauerwin's socks. The test linked Melanson to the murder of Charlotte Sauerwin. Louisiana detectives visited him at the Correctional Facility in Fort Lyon, Colorado, and obtained buccal swabs for DNA testing. On May 27, 2010, the Louisiana State Crime Laboratory confirmed that Melanson's DNA sample matched that found on the sock, and an arrest warrant was issued. That warrant remained outstanding pending completion of the Anita Andrews murder prosecution in Napa, California.

As Napa investigators gradually unearthed Melanson's cruel and twisted criminal history, Prosecutor Paul Gero realized that if he could succeed in getting that history admitted in court, it would be extremely powerful evidence in his case. It clearly illustrated Melanson's predisposition to commit sex crimes. However, Gero knew there would be a legal battle to present these past crimes to a jury. Applicable case law and statutes both allowed and limited the admission of evidence of such prior acts. But that would have to wait until if, and when, this case went to trial. Then there would be a hearing before a judge to determine admissibility of prior "bad acts."

If the judge excluded using these past crimes, would the prosecution still have enough evidence to convict Melanson by the legal standard of "beyond a reasonable doubt"? Gero and his team needed to evaluate their case as if Melanson's prior acts would *not* come into evidence. However, even without this evidence, the trial team still believed they had a strong case against the suspect.

They believed the evidence would show that Melanson had sexually assaulted, beaten, stabbed and murdered Anita Andrews at Fagiani's Cocktail Lounge on the evening of July 10, 1974. They were certain they could show that the screwdriver found behind the bar was the primary murder weapon. The bloody bar towel located on the floor behind the bar

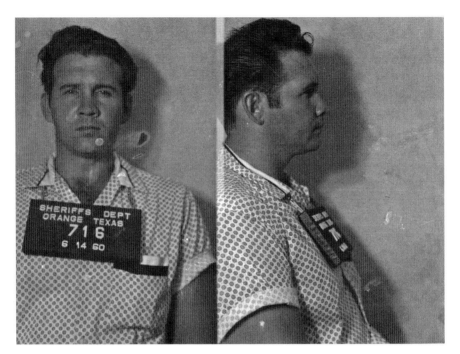

A 1960 mug shot of Roy Melanson from the Orange, Texas Sheriff's Department. *Courtesy of the Napa County District Attorney's Office.*

showed a mixture of DNA from both Anita Andrews and Roy Melanson. They hoped they would be able to raise the inference that Melanson, from behind the bar, had used the towel to clean Anita's blood off himself and wipe blood and fingerprints off the screwdriver. The prosecution team would hammer on the incontrovertible facts that Melanson's DNA evidence placed him at the Napa crime scene, and he was the last person seen with Anita Andrews on the evening of her murder.

The team knew they could prove that Melanson had then fled to Crested Butte, Colorado, where on August 29, 1974, he befriended Michele Wallace. Shortly thereafter, her mother reported her missing. Michele was later found dead, and Roy Melanson was convicted of her murder, which had occurred approximately fifty days after the July 1974 murder of Anita Andrews.

This would be the roadmap for Gero's case. It wasn't what a prosecutor would call a slam-dunk case, but Gero decided there was sufficient circumstantial evidence, plus the DNA evidence placing Melanson at the crime scene, to mount a credible prosecution. The team also recognized their biggest weakness: could someone else have entered the bar after Melanson left?

A 1975 mug shot of Roy Melanson from the Orange, Texas Sheriff's Department. *Courtesy of the Napa County District Attorney's Office.*

But based on the evidence the team had come up with, including the litany of Melanson's criminal conduct in Colorado, Texas and Louisiana, the prosecution team was confident they had identified Anita Andrews's killer. Gero decided to initiate the formal prosecution by filing for a criminal indictment of Roy Melanson for first-degree murder.

18

THE *CASE OF PEOPLE VS. ROY ALLEN MELANSON* GOES TO COURT

Paul Gero had two paths available to him to initiate the prosecution. He could file a criminal complaint, where a judge would decide at a public court hearing whether there existed sufficient or probable cause that the crime had been committed and that the defendant is guilty of that crime. If the judge finds probable cause that the defendant committed the crime, the case may proceed to trial. The defense is present at the hearing and can cross-examine the witnesses presented.

The other path Gero could take was to seek a criminal indictment before a grand jury for the charge of murder. The defendant and the defense attorney are not present. The proceedings are secret and are not held in the context of an adversary proceeding. The grand jury would be composed of county citizens. Grand jurors see and hear only what prosecutors put before them, although the prosecution does have an obligation to present "exculpatory" evidence—evidence that suggests a defendant might not be guilty. In part because there's no one on the "other side" to contest the prosecutor's evidence, grand juries almost always return an indictment as requested by the prosecutor. If an indictment is returned, then the case can proceed to trial.

Gero decided he would start the case with the grand jury, and he presented his murder case to them. On October 6, 2010, the grand jury returned a criminal indictment against Roy Melanson. At the first court hearing on October 19, 2010, a copy of the indictment was handed to Melanson and his appointed counsel, Napa deputy public defender Allison D. Wilensky. On behalf of the defendant, Wilensky acknowledged receipt of the indictment.

Wilensky and her client waived formal reading of the full indictment into the court record. They also waived Melanson's right to be advised of his various trial rights with respect to the charge of murder in the first degree.

Allison Wilensky graduated from Sarah Lawrence College in 1987. She attended Loyola Law School, where she clerked for an attorney whose practice was devoted to death penalty defense cases. In her last year of law school, she received the American Jurisprudence Award for Trial Advocacy. Wilensky graduated from law school in 1990, and in early 1991 she began her law career at the Los Angeles Public Defender's Office. In June 1998, she moved to Northern California to join the Napa County Public Defender's Office.

Deputy Public Defender Allison Wilensky. *Courtesy of Allison Wilensky.*

Wilensky had plenty of trial experience coming into the Melanson trial, having represented clients in approximately sixty misdemeanor and felony jury trials, including dozens of homicide cases.

Wilensky entered a plea of not guilty on Melanson's behalf, and the case was set for trial. However, before the actual trial would occur, the parties would first endeavor to shape the upcoming proceedings by filing a series of preliminary motions.

One of the first motions was a prosecution motion requesting the court's approval to conduct a conditional examination of David Luce. Luce was terminally ill, and it was unclear whether he would live long enough to be present at the trial. To preserve his testimony in the event of his death, Gero asked the court to allow Luce to testify before the trial, on the record, including direct questioning by the prosecution and cross-examination by the defense attorney. If Luce died before the trial date, his testimony would be preserved and allowed in evidence at the trial.

The motion was granted. Investigator Leslie Severe drove to Chico to transport David Luce to Napa. The conditional examination was conducted on November 17, 2010, in Napa Superior Court, with Gero questioning David Luce under oath. Wilensky conducted the cross-examination. Judge Mark Boessenecker presided over the examination and ordered the transcript

The *Napa Valley Register*, September 12, 2010. "Melanson Pleads Not Guilty in Killing at Fagiani's." *Napa County Newspaper Archive.*

to be sealed, which meant that nothing occurring during the examination could be discussed without the court's order. The transcript would be opened and used only if Luce were unable to appear in court.

The defense then filed a motion to continue the trial date—that is, to postpone and reschedule the trial. It was a common motion, allowing the attorneys additional time to properly prepare their cases. The prosecution did not oppose the motion, and the court changed the trial date from May 9, 2011, to September 19, 2011.

On July 5, 2011, Judge Boessenecker assigned the case to Superior Court judge Raymond A. Guadagni for all purposes, which meant that from that date forward, all matters involving the case would be heard by Guadagni as the trial judge. The statutory time period for objection to the court's appointment of the trial judge elapsed with neither Gero nor Wilensky filing an objection.

The case was ready to proceed.

19

BEFORE THE TRIAL

Now that the case was assigned to a trial judge and a trial date set, Wilensky began to move through the checklist of measures that any competent defense lawyer would consider as she developed her strategy for a murder case. Her first step was to move the court for dismissal of the entire indictment on the grounds that it was largely based on hearsay evidence.

MOTION TO DISMISS BECAUSE OF INADMISSIBLE EVIDENCE AND OMITTED EVIDENCE

Hearsay evidence is when a witness tells the court about what other people have said for the purpose of proving the truth of what the other people were talking about. While there are many exceptions to the "hearsay rule," American jurisprudence generally prefers to have the person who saw something actually appear in court, where both sides can examine them, rather than have their information relayed by a third party who may or may not have understood what was said or be able to discern whether the original speaker was lying.

Arguing her motion in a pretrial hearing, Wilensky asserted that the case that the prosecution had presented to the grand jury was riddled with inadmissible hearsay. For example, she said Joe Silva had testified to hearsay regarding the murder victim's habits and whether there were any men involved in her life.

Wilensky also argued that the prosecutor is required to reveal exculpatory evidence to the grand jury. Exculpatory evidence is information that materially diminishes a defendant's blame or fault. Wilensky pointed out that the grand jury had not been told witness David Luce had originally identified *two* men from a photo lineup as possible suspects. They were not told Luce had said to police that on the evening of the crime he did not really look closely at the man in Fagiani's bar and that he did not think he could identify that person.

Wilensky went on to point out other instances of exculpatory evidence that the prosecution had failed to present to the grand jury. The jury was told by an evidence technician that all proper procedures had been followed in the collection and handling of the physical evidence at the crime scene, when in fact certain evidence (including scrapings from the victim's fingernails) had been mishandled. The jury had not been told that the analysis of Melanson's handwriting was inconclusive. Such errors, she argued, deprived Melanson of his due process rights.

Prosecuting attorney Gero appeared at the hearing to oppose Wilensky's motion to dismiss. He responded that Joe Silva's testimony about the victim's habits was fully admissible because Silva had personal knowledge of those habits. He argued the evidence technician's testimony that normal protocol had been followed was admissible because that is what the technician believed. And he asserted that any irregularity in the handling of the scrapings taken from the victim's fingernails was irrelevant because the samples revealed no male DNA.

Gero turned to Wilensky's challenge of David Luce's identification of Roy Melanson on the basis of the photo lineup. He argued that Luce's inability to identify Melanson in the original photo lineups was hardly evidence of his inability to identify the perpetrator because Melanson's photo hadn't even been included in those lineups. And, more importantly, he asserted the whole question of Luce's testimony and the photo lineup didn't matter because the indictment wasn't based on them. The indictment rested on the fact that Melanson's DNA and fingerprints were found at the crime scene.

After reviewing the briefs filed and considering the arguments of both attorneys, Judge Guadagni denied Wilensky's motion to dismiss the indictment.

Motion to Dismiss Because of Prosecution Delay

Undeterred, Wilensky immediately filed another motion to dismiss the indictment, this time on the grounds of prosecution delay, asserting the thirty-seven-year lapse between the initial reporting of the crime and the filing of the indictment was excessive. She cited the death of an important potential witness, Paul Grenier, who had identified a person from a photo lineup who he had said looked exactly like the man seen driving the victim's car after the murder but who was not the same person David Luce had identified.

Anticipating the prosecution's argument that the long delay was because Melanson's DNA was only linked to the crime scene in 2009, Wilensky capped her argument with the assertion that the state's failure to make the DNA comparison until 2009 amounted to negligence.

Gero responded that even if the witnesses cited by Wilensky were still alive, he asserted that their memories would have faded, and the DNA evidence that became available to the prosecution linked only Melanson to the crime scene. Any possible prejudice was lacking in substance.

After hearing oral arguments, Judge Guadagni denied the motion, finding it too speculative to conclude that the testimony of Grenier or any other witness identified in Wilensky's brief would have aided the prosecution. While recognizing that a missing witness might provide relevant testimony, the judge determined that overall prejudice against the defendant was slight because of the existing DNA evidence. Therefore, the delay in bringing the case to prosecution had not impermissibly prejudiced the defendant's constitutional right to due process. Justification for the thirty-seven-year lapse was strong because law enforcement agencies had no basis to suspect the defendant until 2009, when comparison of Melanson's DNA to that found at the crime scene had resulted in a match. Only then did the prosecution have sufficient evidence to charge the defendant. In other words, the delay was due to the slow progress of the investigation. There was no evidence of any effort to delay for the purpose of gaining a tactical advantage, nor was there any basis for the assertion that the prosecution would have had reason to pursue the DNA comparison before 2009.

Pretrial [*In Limine*] Motions

In limine motions are pretrial motions in which the prosecution and defense attorneys can ask the judge to make rulings on certain aspects of the case before a trial begins. Some motions deal with the ground rules of how the trial will proceed; others deal with what evidence will be admissible at trial. Because allowing or disallowing certain evidence could slant a case in favor of one party, these pretrial motions are often strenuously argued by the attorneys.

Prosecutor Gero opened the *in limine* phase of the pretrial process by filing a raft of these motions, asking the court to rule:

1. That the conditional (pretrial) examination of David Luce should be admitted should Luce become unavailable to testify. This motion was granted.
2. That if the defendant testified, evidence of his other crimes of moral turpitude should be admitted. Wilensky responded by pointing out that, if the defendant did not testify, the matter would be moot. She accordingly asked the court to defer consideration of the motion until it became certain the defendant would be testifying. The judge granted Wilensky's request.
3. That photographs of the victim at the crime scene and the coroner's office be admitted into evidence. Wilensky asked the judge to allow her to reserve objections to this motion until she could see which photographs Gero intended to offer. The judge granted Wilensky's request.
4. That when selecting the jury instructions regarding the standards for how evidence was to be evaluated by the jury, the court issue the standards most onerous to the prosecution. For example, in 1974 the crime of rape required there be a showing that the victim resisted or was prevented from resisting. Under current law, no such showing is required. To ensure that the defendant's substantive rights are not violated by substituting a more severe standard *ex post facto* (formulated after 1974), the jury must be instructed according to the 1974 standard. Wilensky asked the judge to reserve argument on this issue until all of the evidence could be evaluated by the judge to determine what proper instructions should be given to the jury. The judge granted Wilensky's request, deferring the decision on the jury instructions.
5. That the jury be allowed to visit the crime scene at some point during the trial. The judge granted this request.

6. That witnesses who had not yet testified be excluded from the courtroom, so they cannot hear the testimony of other witnesses. The judge granted this request.

7. That attorneys not make any speaking objections (one that contains more information than the judge needs to sustain or overrule) in the presence of the jury. The judge granted this request.

Many of Wilensky's pretrial motions on behalf of the defendant overlapped those of Gero, and most of them had already been granted or deferred. However, there was one such motion that proved to be the most bitterly fought of all the pretrial motions. It was the issue of an uncharged crime being allowed as evidence. An "uncharged crime" means that it is either a past or subsequent offense to the one charged in the current court case. Here, only the Andrews murder was the charged crime. Melanson's other crimes were "uncharged" for the purposes of this trial. A judge may allow evidence of one or more uncharged incidents to provide context for the charged incident that is before the jury. Wilensky wanted *all* uncharged crimes excluded from evidence.

Gero countered that evidence of uncharged acts relevant to prove a fact other than bad character or criminal disposition should be allowed to assist the jury in inferring intent. Uncharged crimes of rape would show Melanson's propensity to commit such a crime.

A contentious battle ensued between the attorneys in written briefs and oral arguments over whether Melanson's uncharged offenses should be allowed into evidence before the jury. Both attorneys had legal precedent on their side, and both knew that the outcome of the motion could have a major effect on the trial. Ultimately, the prosecution moved to admit evidence of seven uncharged acts.

The judge ruled that evidence of four of those seven incidents could be offered in evidence during the trial: (1) the 1962 rape of Rhonda T., (2) the 1972 rape of Katherine Ortiz, (3) the 1974 rape of Sandra Arnold and (4) the 1974 murder of Michele Wallace.

The judge ruled against allowing the introduction of evidence of three other uncharged crimes, including: (1) the June 1962 sexual assault of Sandra Chisholm, Melanson's sixteen-year-old cousin; (2) the July 1988 disappearance and presumed murder of Pauline Klumpp; and (3) the 1988 sexual assault and murder of Charlotte Sauerwin.

The judge excluded evidence of the Sandra Chisholm sexual assault because this case would be unduly prejudicial in that Chisholm was only sixteen years old, was a cousin of Melanson's and was molested. Also, Melanson was never convicted of this charge, and there was concern that the jury could wish to punish him for this incident. The judge excluded the presumed murder of Pauline Klumpp because no body was ever found and there was no evidence of sexual assault except for inadmissible hearsay evidence. The 1988 sexual assault and murder of Charlotte Sauerwin was excluded because there was no trial, and introduction of the evidence would result in an undue consumption of time to prove this crime, resulting in a mini-trial conducted before the Melanson jury. There was also a concern that the jury would punish Melanson because there had been no conviction in that case.

Gero and his trial team considered the ruling on the motion a major victory. The jury would learn about four previous acts that showed Melanson's propensity for sexual assault and violence against women, plus his intent and modus operandi.

20

A SURPRISE WITNESS

T he trial was set to begin on September 19, 2011, in Department G of the Criminal Court Building on Third Street in Napa, less than one block from Fagiani's bar. Department G is known as the ceremonial courtroom because it has the largest audience capacity (approximately seventy people). As a result, high-profile cases were usually tried there.

The courtroom was not packed on that September morning because one hundred prospective jurors were waiting across the street in the jury assembly room. In the courtroom, Judge Guadagni and attorneys Gero and Wilensky were discussing aspects of the upcoming jury selection process. They then walked across the street to the jury assembly room to instruct the jury on filling out the hardship questionnaire, by which a prospective juror could request to be excused from jury duty because of medical, economic or some other hardship. Hardship excusals were not automatically granted, but in a trial anticipated to last two weeks or longer, such requests were always given careful consideration.

In all, over a dozen prospective jurors requested to be excused. Judge Guadagni granted most of these requests on grounds ranging from physical health issues to the logistical challenges of a single parent. The judge then ordered a recess to allow the attorneys time to review the long-form questionnaires filled out by the remaining prospective jurors. Running eleven pages with thirty-four questions, this questionnaire elicited information about the prospective jurors' social, educational and professional history, as well as life experiences that might affect a juror's perceptions of the case.

Attorneys use these as a guide in questioning prospective jurors about their background and qualifications to hear a particular case. For example, a prospective juror with a family member who had been raped or murdered might not be suitable for a rape/murder case. Actual jury selection was to begin the following day, September 20, 2011.

Within two minutes of returning to his chambers, the judge received a phone call. "The attorneys want to see you," his clerk said.

"What? We just finished preliminary jury selection. What could they want?"

Both attorneys were conscientious, so the judge thought it must concern something they didn't want on record. But what? He was used to last-minute surprises and requests for postponements, but he wanted to get started on this long-awaited trial.

In a few minutes, the two trial attorneys appeared. Prosecuting attorney Gero started by saying, "Your Honor, we have a witness who was made known to us just this morning."

"And I object," defense attorney Wilensky added. "If you allow this witness to testify this late in the game, the defense will need a continuance to investigate and prepare. Moreover," she continued, "I may have a conflict of interest if I, or any of my colleagues, have represented this person in the past."

"Well," the judge said, "this must be put on the record outside the presence of the jury. I'd better get the court reporter in here."

"Your Honor," Gero said, "both Allison and I want to just talk this out with you off the record because I'm not sure I want to call this witness."

Wilensky agreed. "We should go on the record only if we can't resolve the matter informally."

"Paul, this is late for discovery of a new witness," the judge said. "What took so long to come up with him? Why couldn't this have been disclosed earlier, in the months leading up to the trial?"

"We just found out about the existence of this man. Apparently, last night in the jail Mr. Melanson admitted that he did, in fact, kill the victim and said he was glad he did it. He said this to an inmate, whom we may want to call as a witness. This all came to light last night, and we were told about it only this morning. We haven't been sitting on this disclosure only to surprise the defense with it this morning."

Wilensky agreed. "I'm sure these facts developed just the way Paul says. The only thing is, if you allow this witness to testify, I must have a continuance."

"Paul," the judge said, "do you intend to call this witness or not? If you do, then Ms. Wilensky will request a continuance, and I will have to hear this on the record."

Gero hesitated. "May I go back to my office? I need to confer with my colleagues."

"Okay. If you seek the continuance, we will go on the record, and I will hear arguments from both of you."

But, the judge wondered, why would the prosecuting attorney *not* want to present this witness? Melanson's confession to the crime would be valuable evidence in the quest to convict him. On the other hand, he knew that Gero might be reluctant to call an inmate from the jail as a witness because inmate witnesses are problematic. Such a witness could be trying to get something in return for giving favorable testimony for the prosecution, perhaps seeking leniency in his own sentence in return for his testimony. This could be viewed as possible witness bias, which could affect his credibility. He would have a motive to lie. Also, an inmate witness has been charged with or convicted of some crime, which is why he was in jail. Felonies could be used to impeach a witness's credibility.

Gero might be uncertain whether the witness would stand up to the vigorous cross-examination that Wilensky would surely put him through. Some attorneys believed that if doubt was created about one aspect of the prosecution's case, it could raise doubt about their entire case. Wilensky would surely argue this point if she impeached the inmate's testimony.

At 1:25 p.m., the phone rang in the judge's chambers. Both attorneys wanted to see him.

Gero said he had decided to proceed with his case and not call the inmate witness. Wilensky concurred that the trial could go forward.

The following morning, the prospective jurors were brought into the courtroom, and *voir dire* (jury selection) commenced. By the end of the day, twelve jurors and three alternate jurors had been duly sworn to try the case of *People vs. Roy Allen Melanson*. Before excusing them for the day, the judge admonished them not to discuss the case or form or express an opinion about the case until all the evidence had been presented to them, and then only when all twelve jurors were together in the jury deliberation room.

The trial would start the following day, September 21, 2011.

21

THE TRIAL BEGINS

SEPTEMBER 21, 2011

Thirty-seven years after the brutal slaying of Anita Andrews, Roy Allen Melanson went on trial for her murder. There were surprisingly few spectators in the courtroom on that opening day—a reporter and press photographer from the *Napa Valley Register*, young deputy attorneys from the District Attorney's and Public Defender's Offices there to observe and four members of the general public.

Courtroom observers might have expected the defendant, Roy Melanson, to look like a brutal killer. Instead, people saw an old man in a wheelchair, waiting for deputies to remove the handcuffs from his wrists. Melanson was seventy-four years old, and in his wheelchair he did not appear threatening or evil. The bailiffs and correctional officers who led him into court later said he was pleasant to work with, didn't complain, courteously obeyed their instructions and usually had a smile on his face. Roy Melanson looked more like a kindly grandfather than a cold-blooded killer.

It would be up to the prosecuting attorney to present as much incriminating evidence as possible, and he would have to tie that evidence together with testimony from witnesses and forensic experts to convince the jury of Melanson's guilt beyond a reasonable doubt. This evidence would have to speak for Anita Andrews.

The jury had been selected, and the judge gave preliminary instructions regarding presumption of innocence and what constitutes reasonable doubt. Then the judge allowed the prosecuting and defense attorneys to give their opening statements of what he or she believes the evidence will show the jury. The prosecution, which has the burden of proof, goes first.

At 9:30 a.m. on September 21, 2011, prosecuting attorney Paul Gero walked slowly to a spot a few feet in front of the jury, looked directly at them and began.

"This case is about the brutal murder of an innocent woman and the fine detective work and advances in forensic science that have allowed this crime to be solved thirty-seven years later. In 1974, Anita Andrews was a fifty-one-year-old divorced mother of two, working two jobs. During the day she worked as a secretary and typist at Napa State Hospital, and in the evenings, she worked as a bartender at Fagiani's Cocktail Lounge, located at 813 Main Street in downtown Napa, just a block from here. After her shift at the hospital Anita would drive her tan 1967 Cadillac over to the bar, park that Cadillac right in front, and work there for about four hours.

"On Wednesday, July 10, 1974, Anita Andrews went to work at Fagiani's bar as usual. During that evening, David Luce and two friends entered the bar around closing time, and inside they saw two people: Anita Andrews, who was working behind the bar, and someone Luce and his friends had never seen before, a Caucasian adult male in his forties with a wet hairstyle and thin lips, seated directly across from Anita. He was smoking and had a bottle of beer in front of him, and he and Anita were engaged in quiet conversation.

"Anita Andrews was never seen alive again.

"Because Anita had not returned home that night, the next morning her sister, Muriel, went to Fagiani's bar looking for her. In the back stockroom she found Anita lying in a pool of blood with her clothes mostly ripped off. Muriel called the police.

"Napa Police Officer Joe Moore arrived at the scene first. He conducted analysis of the crime scene, collected evidence, and took photographs. Later, Criminalist Peter Barnett also collected evidence and took a lot more photographs.

"Three pieces of significant evidence were collected from that crime scene. One was a recently washed, still wet screwdriver lying on top of the bar that tested positive for blood. The second piece of important evidence was a bar towel that had been tossed behind the bar. That tested positive for blood as well. The third piece of evidence was an ashtray containing one cigarette butt. That cigarette butt was saved for the next thirty-seven years.

"Barnett noted that Anita Andrews looked as if she had been the victim of a sexual assault or an attempted sexual assault. He also noted that her tan Cadillac was not parked in front as it usually was.

"The pathologist will tell you that Anita Andrews had three primary injuries. The first was blunt force trauma to her face, nose and lip, as well as contusions, a laceration to her scalp, and what is called a subdural hematoma, which is bleeding from the brain. Her skull was fractured, and fragments of glass were found in her hair. The cause of death was thirteen stab wounds to the left side of her body, extending from her lung all the way up to her neck.

"The two lead investigators at the time did everything they could to solve this case, but they could not identify the stranger in the bar, and they never did find the Cadillac. They did collect a rum bottle and some beer bottles from the bar, as well as a receipt from Cristoni's Phillips 66 truck stop gas station in Sacramento, where Anita's credit card had been used to purchase gasoline on July 11, the morning after her death. The signature on the credit card receipt read 'A. Andrews.'

"But the unidentified stranger could not be found, and the case went cold for the next thirty-seven years. However, the Napa Police Department never gave up, and neither did Muriel Fagiani. In 2001, the case was reopened by Pete Jerich, a Napa police detective who sent that bloody bar towel I just mentioned for testing at the Department of Justice Crime Lab in Sacramento. And then in 2006, because of new advances in forensic science, Detective Don Winegar sent the cigarette butt found at the crime scene to the Department of Justice for testing.

"You will hear testimony in this case from DNA specialists who will tell you that the DNA profile from analysis of that cigarette butt matched that of the defendant, Roy Allen Melanson. In addition, a private crime lab conducted a DNA analysis that found the DNA on the bloody bar towel matched the DNA profile of Roy Allen Melanson.

"You will also hear testimony from a fingerprint expert who compared fingerprints collected from the five beer bottles and one rum bottle at the crime scene with those of Mr. Melanson and found a total of fifteen matches. In addition, a handwriting expert compared the gas receipt signed 'A. Andrews' with a handwriting sample from Roy Melanson and found similarities.

"Mr. Melanson was then interviewed in person by Detective Don Winegar. When asked about the murder of Anita Andrews, Mr. Melanson said, 'I don't know anything about it.' When Detective Winegar brought up the DNA and fingerprint evidence, Mr. Melanson said, 'DNA is wrong, fingerprints are wrong, everything's wrong. It wasn't me. I've never been to Fagiani's bar. In fact, I've never been to Napa in my entire life. I have no involvement in this case.' He denied everything. But the evidence, ladies and gentlemen, will prove otherwise.

"During the trial you will learn something about Mr. Melanson's background, which includes evidence of several rapes, and a murder which occurred in Gunnison, Colorado on August 30, 1974, less than 60 days after the murder of Anita Andrews."

Gero drew a slow breath and concluded his statement by saying, "Based on this evidence, at the conclusion of the trial I will ask you to find the defendant, Roy Allen Melanson, guilty of the murder of Anita Andrews."

It was now defense attorney Allison Wilensky's turn to make an opening statement. She took Gero's place at the podium in front of the jury, looked at the jury members and then began.

"This trial will probably not last as long as you've been told, and that's a good thing. This is a reasonable-doubt case. The prosecutor has told you what he thinks he's going to prove. While he's attempting to prove these things, you will be hearing other pieces of evidence that he hasn't told you about, and you will also not be hearing certain things that one would think you could hear.

"It is pretty clear that Mr. Melanson was in that bar, and it's pretty clear that the DNA will show you that he smoked that cigarette. However, the evidence will not show you who came into the bar or who didn't come into the bar after David Luce and his two friends left. In fact, the evidence is going to demonstrate that it is entirely unclear what time those three men did leave. The evidence is not going to show you that Mr. Melanson was the last person in the bar because there's no way of knowing that and no way of knowing if Mr. Melanson was that man on the barstool.

"You will hear from Mr. Luce. And you will hear that over the course of thirty-seven years he has identified other photographs of persons he thought could have been the suspect in the bar. You will see pictures of composites and maybe an actual photograph put together based on a description of everyone who talked about that last man in the bar, and you will see that those descriptions do not match Mr. Melanson. And you will be able to see that for yourself."

Wilensky then continued with her goal of casting doubt on the forensic evidence. "You will hear about the DNA found on the cigarette. You will also hear that Mr. Melanson's DNA was found on a bloody towel. And while you will hear testimony that the DNA sample from the towel *could* belong to Mr. Melanson, you will also hear testimony that the DNA sample matches 1 in 700 people.

"You will also hear testimony about the screwdriver said to be the murder weapon. But there are no fingerprints on that screwdriver. There is no DNA. In other words, you will hear testimony *only* that Mr. Melanson was present at Fagiani's bar on the night of July 10, 1974, but no testimony about what occurred. You will also hear that, while there were some similarities between Mr. Melanson's handwriting and the handwriting on the gasoline receipt, there were elements in both writing samples that did not match at all."

Wilensky then paused, looked at the jury and said, "Reasonable doubt." After a weighty pause, she continued by saying: "You will hear testimony about the Colorado homicide, and you will be instructed as to how you are to consider that. You will be listening for details about how that crime in Colorado was committed, and the prosecutor will ask you to compare that information to this crime.

"Regarding the rape that you're going to hear about, you will hear about a conviction, but you will be reading the transcript of the rape of Katherine Ortiz. This is not a conviction. You will see no evidence of a conviction. This is testimony from a woman who describes her rape, but when asked to identify the person who had raped her, identified someone in a courtroom who was not Mr. Melanson."

Allison Wilensky concluded her opening statement by saying, "These are the pieces of evidence in this reasonable-doubt case that you're going to hear, and when we're all done, I'm going to ask you to seriously think about what reasonable doubt is, and I'll ask you to return a verdict of not guilty."

Wilensky then turned and walked back to her seat at the defense table next to Melanson.

The opening statements had made one thing clear to every person in the court room. The case was not clear-cut for either the prosecution or the defense. The jury would need to see and hear from the witnesses themselves to determine if there was reasonable doubt.

22

TESTIMONIES OF THOSE FIRST ON THE MURDER SCENE

SEPTEMBER 21, 2011

NAPA POLICE OFFICERS JOSEPH FRANCIS MOORE AND LIEUTENANT JOHN E. BAILEY

The first witness prosecuting attorney Gero called was retired Napa police officer Joseph Moore, who was on uniformed patrol duty on July 11, 1974. Officer Moore testified that he heard a radio dispatch call requesting available patrol officers to go to Fagiani's bar on a "coroner's case," which alerted the officer receiving the call that a fatality was involved. He was the first officer on the crime scene.

Moore recalled that when he entered the bar, Muriel Fagiani led him to the back storage room, where he saw the body of Anita Andrews on the floor. Her clothing was in disarray, and blood was on the floor around her upper torso. Moore tried to get Muriel to move to the front door so he could secure the crime scene, but she didn't want to leave her sister. Then Police Sergeant Don Kemper arrived, and the two officers secured the crime scene and called the coroner. Shortly thereafter, Captain Dewey Burnsed and Lieutenant John Bailey arrived and were able to coax Muriel from the bar into Moore's patrol car.

At that point, Moore determined that Anita's Cadillac was missing, so at 9:30 a.m., he issued an all-points bulletin to alert all police units throughout the state of California about the missing car.

This concluded Officer Moore's testimony for the prosecution. Gero had succeeded in selecting an initial witness who had been able to quickly and clearly set the scene for the jury and create a foundation for the diverse

Left: Napa police officer Joe Moore was the first officer to arrive at the crime scene in 1974. He testified at the 2011 trial of Roy Melanson. *Courtesy of the Napa Police Historical Society.*

Right: Napa police lieutenant John Bailey. *Courtesy of the Napa Police Historical Society.*

information to come. Moore's demeanor on the stand had been calm, straightforward and convincing.

Defense attorney Wilensky cross-examined Moore about his actions at the crime scene, but she quickly realized his testimony was not damaging to the defendant or his credibility, so her cross-examination was brief.

Gero then called Lieutenant John Bailey, one of the first officers on the scene. He testified that he was assigned to lead the investigation along with Lieutenant Robert Jarecki, and he recalled that the forensic experts were gathering and examining potential evidence. Bailey then set out to locate the victim's 1967 Cadillac.

On July 15, he returned to the bar to collect additional evidence, including a rum bottle found on the floor by Anita's body and a number of beer bottles. These were turned over to criminalist Peter Barnett.

Gero then asked about a credit card purchase in Sacramento on the day after Anita's murder. Lieutenant Bailey remembered that in August 1974, a few weeks after the murder, a staff investigator for Bank of America reported that Anita Andrews's credit card had been used to purchase gasoline at the V.E. Cristoni Phillips 66 truck stop, and that sale had been for the purchase of fuel for a 1967 Cadillac with a license number that matched that of Anita's vehicle. Bailey testified that he drove to Sacramento and interviewed the gas station employee, who said he had sold the gasoline to a man driving a tan 1967 Cadillac. He gave Bailey the paper receipt, and Bailey booked that receipt into evidence at the Napa Police Department.

Wilensky probed and probed but found no weakness in Bailey's testimony or in his unshakable demeanor.

Criminalist Peter D. Barnett

Thirty-seven years after examining the crime scene as a young criminalist, Peter Barnett now took the witness stand for the prosecution. In a cold case of such long duration, it is rare for the original criminalist who reconstructed the crime to still be practicing and available to testify at trial. Barnett was twenty-seven years old when he traveled from Berkeley to Napa to inspect and reconstruct the scene of Anita Andrews's murder. Now sixty-four, he was on the witness stand to testify about his findings when he had examined and analyzed the physical evidence at the crime scene.

Gero presented Barnett to the jury as an expert witness in the field of criminalistics and crime scene reconstruction. An expert witness must have special knowledge, training, education and experience in his field. Barnett had graduated from the University of California at Berkeley in 1968 with a bachelor of science degree in criminalistics. He had worked for Paul Kirk and Associates in Berkeley, a consulting firm in the field of criminalistics, and then for the San Diego Police Department before opening his own office. In 1978, Barnett and a colleague had formed Forensic Science Associates.

Barnett was a member of the California Association of Criminalists and the criminalistics section of the American Academy of Forensic Sciences. He had been published in the field of criminalistics and authored a book on the subject. In addition, Barnett had appeared as an expert witness in courts throughout California as well as in Washington, Oregon, Nevada, Arizona, Texas, Colorado and Oklahoma. He had also testified in federal courts in Guam and California.

Much of Barnett's testimony consisted of identifying the many photographs he took at the scene. He had also made sketches of the scene and taken detailed measurements of the bar itself, the barstools, pool table, other customer tables and the area behind the bar. His testimony created the foundation for the admission of numerous photographs and measurements of the storage room where the body was found. He described the exact location of the body as well as blood spatters on the walls and blood traces on other items in the room, including the screwdriver found on the sink in the bar.

Defense attorney Wilensky had wanted no graphic photos shown to the jury, and when the prosecution moved for introduction of the first such photos during Barnett's testimony, Wilensky objected. She reminded the judge that she had asked him to reserve ruling on her motion to exclude photographs until she could see exactly what photographs Paul Gero would offer in evidence. Accordingly, the judge excused the jury from the courtroom and then heard arguments from both attorneys.

Wilensky asked the judge to exclude from jury consideration photographs depicting the vivid, shocking violence perpetrated on the victim. Gero argued that these photographs demonstrated what had physically happened to Anita Andrews and the jury should be allowed to view them.

Wilensky countered that such photographs would inflame the passions of the jury, thus creating bias against her client. She argued Barnett's testimony about the nature of the victim's wounds would suffice, so the graphic photos were not needed. Eying the thick stack of enlarged photos on the prosecution table waiting to be offered into evidence, she went on to argue that the large number of photographs showing the condition of the victim's body were not necessary.

The judge held Gero's argument about the relevance of the graphic photos to be valid and went on to allow some, but not all, of the photographs into evidence. However, he shared the defense's concerns about the volume of graphic photos proposed for admission. He limited them to those that were necessary to illustrate the condition of the victim's body and its position in relation to blood spatter and other items of evidence in the storage room.

The jury returned to the courtroom. Barnett hypothesized that the victim may have hit her head as she fell onto a wooden crate and trash can in the storage room. He also described in detail the tears and rips in her clothing.

Gero then asked Barnett about the screwdriver. Barnett testified that the nature of the stab wounds indicated this was the murder weapon and noted that the state of the victim's clothing indicated a struggle with her assailant. He took about eighty photographs of the crime scene and tested items for the presence of blood. He also said he found no purse, pocketbook or credit cards.

He then turned to the postmortem examination by the coroner, Dr. David Clary, at Claffey and Rota Funeral Home on the afternoon of July 11, 1974.

Barnett said he took approximately twenty photographs during the autopsy and also collected the victim's fingerprints and fingernail clippings.

Gero then asked about his analysis of the crime scene reconstruction. Barnett testified that the blood pattern outside the storage room door indicated the initial injury to the victim had occurred outside the storage room, but she then moved into the storage room, where another struggle took place. At some point, she was struck on the head with the bottle that was found shattered on the storage room floor. Anita's head briefly rested on the Lucky Lager box in the storage room; then she slid down, and her head came to rest against the garbage can. From there, she slid on down to the floor, where she was repeatedly stabbed along her left side.

Barnett testified that he saw no evidence of more than one attacker, but there was a possible sexual assault or attempted sexual assault, although no semen was detected. The victim was found lying on her back, partially unclothed, wearing pantyhose and a pair of pants that were entirely off her right leg but remained on her left leg. Her girdle and panties had been removed from her right leg. Her vagina was exposed. Her blouse had been opened completely and her brassiere pulled down, exposing her breasts. One shoe was on, the other off.

Examination of the body showed no indication that sexual intercourse had actually occurred, but Barnett testified, "The condition of the clothing speaks for itself."

Gero posed a hypothetical question: "Assuming that the assailant used the screwdriver as the murder weapon and that the victim's blood is on the towel underneath the sink, do you believe that the assailant went to the sink to clean himself off after leaving the storage room?"

Barnett answered, "I believe that, yes." He concluded his direct testimony that, based on blood he observed on the inside of the front door, he believed the assailant left through the front door of the bar.

Defense attorneys have a number of strategies available for the cross-examination of prosecution witnesses. They will, of course, always be alert for opportunities to throw doubt on the validity of testimony that directly implicates their client in the crime. Beyond that, however, they will often question matters that, on their face, are not directly connected to the proof of guilt. The goal is to show the jury that testimony can never be accepted at face value; the jury's responsibility is to constantly be evaluating the accuracy and weight of what it is hearing.

Wilensky began her cross-examination of Barnett on this tack, asking several questions designed to point out to the jury that Barnett had testified on a number of points relating to the crime scene that were not shown in the photographs that had been introduced into evidence. While none of these questions exposed contradictions in the presented evidence, they showed the jury that some of Barnett's testimony was based on his thirty-seven-year-old memory rather than a graphic record.

Wilensky's questioning then turned to the fact that Barnett, in his testimony, had referred to "the assailant."

"Is there anything that you saw that suggests it had to be only one person?"

"No," Barnett replied. "There could have been other people there, but what their involvement might have been, I couldn't say."

Wilensky pursued this point, asking, "So is it fair to say that, based on your crime scene reconstruction, you don't know how many people were involved, other than at least one assailant and the dead woman, correct?"

"Correct."

Wilensky brought up Barnett's previous testimony regarding how long the incident inside the storage room would have taken. When questioned by Gero, Barnett had testified that the incident "would have taken some period of time." In a brief series of questions, Wilensky was able to get Barnett to agree that the incident might have taken only a few minutes, or it might have extended over a period of hours.

"Can you narrow it down at all?" she asked.

"No, it's hard," Barnett responded.

Wilensky switched to the topic of a bottle that had been found at the crime scene on the stairway leading from the bar area to the upstairs office. "Do you recall that bottle?" she asked.

Barnett replied he did not recall that bottle.

Wilensky showed him a photograph that had been offered into evidence by the prosecution. It showed the stairway and the single bottle resting on one of the steps.

She asked Barnett if he could see the bottle in the photo. Barnett said yes. She asked him if he had collected that particular bottle as evidence. Barnett said he had not.

Wilensky ended her cross-examination by asking Barnett if that bottle, which he did not collect as evidence, was close to the stair on which he had found blood.

"Yes," he responded. "That bottle was in the general area of the stairs that had blood on them." He went on to say he believed the bottle was on the third stair, while the blood was on the second and fourth stairs.

As Wilensky finished her cross-examination, it was becoming apparent to Gero that her questions regarding the bottle might have succeeded in creating doubt in the jurors' minds regarding the thoroughness of Barnett's entire investigation. Gero accordingly rose for redirect examination.

Gero asked Barnett whether the collection of evidence such as the bottle had been assigned to Sergeant Chuck Hansen. Barnett replied that Sergeant Hansen's assignment was to collect items for fingerprinting; Barnett's job was to collect items that were not specifically for fingerprint analysis.

Having provided the jury with a plausible reason for Barnett's not having a recollection of the bottle, Gero apparently decided against drawing more attention to the issue. He told the court he had no further questions.

Wilensky had no further questions, either. Peter Barnett was excused.

23

MORE INCRIMINATING EVIDENCE IS PRESENTED

SEPTEMBER 22, 2011

WITNESS DAVID LUCE

The prosecution opened the second day of trial by calling David Luce to the witness stand. Luce was one of the three friends who had been customers at Fagiani's bar on the night of the murder. He was also the only person in the bar that evening who saw *up close* the man sitting on the bar stool directly across from Anita Andrews. Luce had even shaken the man's hand.

It was a strange scene for the jury. Both Luce and Melanson were in wheelchairs. After thirty-seven years, they sat across the courtroom from each other as the jury watched. Roy Melanson was now seventy-four years old. David Luce was sixty-seven and suffering from terminal cancer.

Luce nevertheless appeared strong and lucid, apparently determined to testify before he died. He often stared in Melanson's direction and periodically turned his upper body toward the defendant and looked directly at him. When asked to point Melanson out in the courtroom, Luce unhesitatingly pointed at the defendant.

During most of Luce's testimony, Melanson sat with his head down, looking at the tabletop. When he occasionally looked up at Luce, it was a blank stare.

Gero began by directing Luce's attention to the evening of the murder when he and his two friends were customers at Fagiani's bar. Gero asked Luce to describe what he saw and what had occurred.

Luce replied that upon entering the bar, he and his two friends had seen a man, whose identity was unknown to them, sitting at the far end of the bar. The man had been smoking a cigarette and shielding his face with his left hand.

"I don't think he said a word," Luce recalled. "He was drinking." He described the man as in his forties with a receding hairline and "thinnish" lips. He was sitting on a bar stool, his legs crossed "like a girl." After one of Luce's friends yelled at the man, Luce wanted to ease the tension, so he went up to him and offered to shake hands.

After all these years, Luce still remembered that handshake, describing it as "just like President Nixon's." He explained he had once shaken the president's hand, and it was "the hottest, softest, wimpiest hand" he had ever shaken. The description drew laughter from the jury.

Luce said he thought Anita might have said the unidentified man was her boyfriend to prevent trouble. He then said that the next morning he heard something had happened at Fagiani's bar the night before, so he immediately called the police. The police interviewed him that same day.

Luce then testified that he had identified Melanson's photograph in January 2010 when Detective Winegar presented a photo lineup. Luce then said the photo he identified was the man he had seen in Fagiani's bar that July evening in 1974.

From the moment she began her cross-examination, it was apparent defense attorney Wilensky was clearly determined to cast doubt on Luce's memory. She cited an interview Luce had had with Officer Mike Roth of the Napa Police Department on July 10, 1975, one year after the murder. Luce had told Roth he "really didn't look at the guy" but rather "kind of looked through him." Referring to another interview with law enforcement, Wilensky asked Luce if he remembered telling Captain Sherman Schulte on October 7, 1975, that he didn't think he could identify the man in the bar. Luce said he did not recall the conversation.

Wilensky then questioned Luce about a photo lineup during an interview conducted in 1974. She pointed out that on March 26, 1990, Luce had told Captain Robert Jarecki that, of the nine men whose photographs were shown to him, photo no. 1 appeared to look most like the unidentified man in the bar and photo no. 8 was Luce's second choice, but he couldn't be sure. Luce responded that he remembered talking to Captain Jarecki but that none of the nine photographs had been of the man in the bar.

Wilensky also elicited testimony from Luce that when he had walked past Fagiani's bar later that evening, after leaving another bar, he really didn't know if the tan Cadillac had been parked in front or not. She then pointed out that this testimony contradicted Luce's prior statements that the car was not there.

Wilensky asked Luce whether he had read newspaper articles about the case provided to him by his ex-wife over the years. At first, Luce testified that his ex-wife would tell him about an article on the internet, but she did not send him articles or newspaper clippings. When Wilensky pointed out that Luce had previously testified he did read the *Napa Register* and that his ex-wife had sent him clippings, Luce then said he recalled his ex-wife "doing that sort of thing."

During redirect examination, Gero asked Luce about his prior photograph identifications. Luce responded that when he selected someone who most resembled the person he had seen in the bar that night, he meant someone who had some characteristics in common with the man he had seen. He did not necessarily mean the person was the actual man he had seen.

Gero concluded by asking Luce to explain his selection of identification photographs over the years. Luce testified that before Detective Winegar showed him his photo lineup in 2010, he had never identified the man he saw in the bar. Winegar's photo lineup "was the first time I ever saw anybody that I thought was the person."

POLICE DETECTIVE PETER JERICH

The next two witnesses Gero presented were crucial in establishing the integrity of test results and were thus important to his overall case. The prosecution had to prove that the evidence had been properly preserved and correctly delivered to the crime laboratory at the Department of Justice in Sacramento. Known as the chain of custody, this foundation was particularly important in a case that had remained cold for over three decades. If the prosecution could not prove the chain of custody, the test results would be open to allegations of tampering or contamination.

The first of these two witnesses was Detective Peter Jerich of the Napa Police Department. Under direct examination by prosecutor Gero, Detective Jerich testified he had been a police officer for twenty-nine years, twenty-six and a half of those with the City of Napa Police Department. In 2000, he attended a training on the investigation of cold case homicides. Shortly after completing the training, he reopened the 1974 homicide of Anita Andrews and submitted pertinent evidence to the Department of Justice in Sacramento for DNA profiling. Jerich testified that he obtained the evidence items from the evidence property room in the Napa Police Department building, and the evidence was packaged, sealed and delivered to the Department of Justice laboratory on December 13, 2001.

Napa police detective Pete Jerich.
Courtesy of the Napa Police Historical Society.

Detective Jerich went on to enumerate the various items of evidence. These included three towels that had been found at the crime scene. There were fingernail clippings and hair samples from the victim. There were also two items of evidence (hair samples and fingerprints) relating to a man named Liston Beal, whom police had at an earlier stage of the investigation identified as a possible suspect. While they had since decided it was unlikely that he had committed the murder, Jerich had submitted the evidence to help confirm their tentative conclusion.

When Wilensky cross-examined Jerich, it was apparent she wanted to cast doubt on the integrity of the evidence. She first asked how the three towels were packaged. Jerich said they were in a brown paper sack, but because the bags were sealed and marked as evidence, he admitted he didn't know whether the towels were encased in plastic bags inside the paper sack.

Wilensky then asked whether the evidence had been stored in a banker's box or just on a shelf in the property room. Jerich answered, "I think they were in the bag, and the bag was inside the box."

She pressed him on this. "Was the evidence stored in a room that is kept at room temperature?"

"Yes," he replied.

She kept prodding. "In a room or in a separate warehouse?"

"They have a main property room and a separate room in a basement area where they keep long-term evidence," Jerich answered. "You have to go through a couple of secured doors, and I know one of them is alarmed. It's kind of like a basement, you know, a little cool in there. But I don't believe it's refrigerated or anything like that."

Wilensky then asked, "Is that the same place the fingernails and hair samples were stored?"

"Yes."

She had no further questions.

POLICE DETECTIVE TODD SHULMAN

To further corroborate the chain of custody, Gero called Detective Todd Shulman. Shulman testified that he had worked with Detective Winegar, and one of his duties was to transport evidence for testing to the Department of Justice in Sacramento. On November 29, 2007, Winegar gave him some evidence, which was sealed, and on that same day Shulman personally transported it by automobile to the DNA laboratory at the Department of Justice in Sacramento. He filled out a property evidence voucher and signed the evidence over to Luis Hermaso, a lab technician, then returned a copy of the voucher to the Napa Police Department.

Napa police detective Todd Shulman. *Courtesy of the Napa Police Historical Society.*

"What specific items of evidence did you deliver to the Department of Justice that day?" Gero asked.

"A screwdriver, some crushed glass, a blood smear, hair and a cigarette butt with ashes."

With no apparent gap in the chain of custody, defense attorney Wilensky had no cross-examination questions.

POLICE DETECTIVE DON WINEGAR

Gero next called Detective Don Winegar. At the time of the trial, he had been a police officer for almost twenty-seven years and a detective for ten years. In May 2006, he was assigned the Andrews murder cold case. Winegar testified that he began by inventorying the evidence kept in storage since 1974 and all the police reports since that time. As he went through

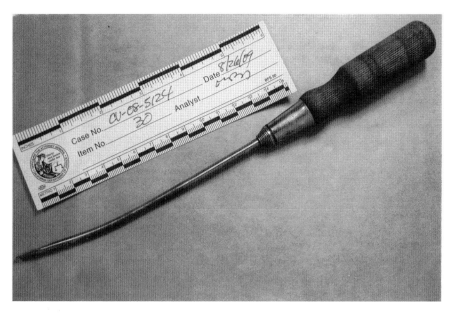

Evidence photo of the screwdriver (murder weapon). *Courtesy of the Napa County District Attorney's Office.*

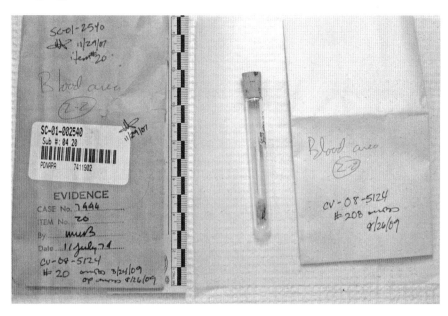

Evidence photo of blood swab. *Courtesy of the Napa County District Attorney's Office.*

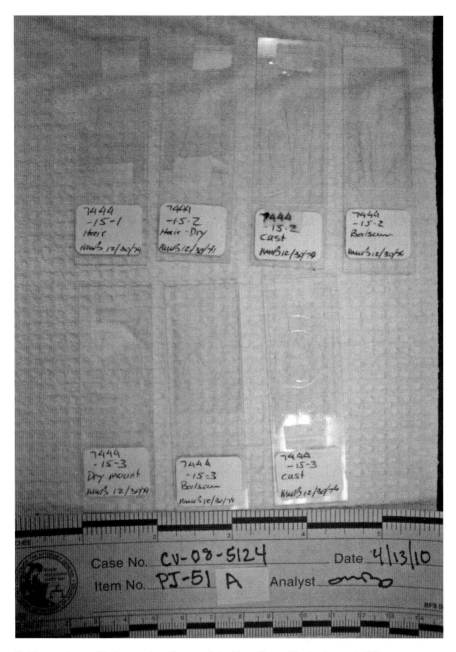

Evidence photo of hair samples. *Courtesy of the Napa County District Attorney's Office.*

the evidence in storage, he realized there were no forensic test results on the evidence submitted to the Department of Justice by Officer Pete Jerich in 2001. Consequently, Winegar contacted the Department of Justice to find out whether the submitted evidence had been tested.

He said he did not hear back from the DOJ criminalist assigned to the case, Michelle Terra, until July 2006 because Terra had been on maternity leave. Upon her return, Winegar authorized additional testing on the towel Officer Jerich had originally sent to the DOJ lab, which resulted in its being sent to the Serological Research Institute (SERI), a private serological testing facility. Winegar testified that in November 2007 he also submitted additional evidence to the DOJ lab, including a cigarette butt with ashes, which had originally been found in the ashtray on the counter of the bar.

Gero asked Winegar if he had received a telephone call from Michelle Terra regarding a DNA match.

"Yes," Winegar said.

"On the cigarette?"

Winegar stated, "Yes, sir." He went on to say that Terra gave him the name of the person identified by the match data, along with other identifying information.

"What was the name?" Gero asked.

"Roy Melanson."

Winegar then authored a search warrant, signed by Napa Superior Court judge Stephen T. Kroyer, around November 24, 2009.

"And did that search warrant order DNA samples, fingerprints and a handwriting sample?"

"Yes," Winegar answered. "It did."

Winegar testified that around November 30, 2009, he traveled to Colorado and met with Roy Melanson, who was in prison.

"Do you see Roy Melanson in the courtroom today?"

"Yes, I do," replied Winegar.

"Would you please point to him, describe what he's wearing today."

Winegar replied, "He's wearing a dress shirt with a tie, and he's sitting to the right of the defense attorney."

Gero then asked if he had collected evidence from Melanson for DNA comparisons. Winegar responded that a certified nurse had collected buccal swabs of the inside of Melanson's mouth and drawn some blood. Winegar said he sealed this evidence, labeled it and delivered it to Michelle Terra at the Department of Justice on December 7, 2009. On January 29, 2010, he delivered additional items of evidence to Terra, who by this time was working at the Central Valley Department of Justice laboratory in Ripon, California. The additional items included hair samples from the scene, the victim's shoe, portions of her pantyhose, a broken bottle, fingernail clippings, other items of clothing and the blood-soaked towel. Then on August 17, 2010, he delivered the sealed towel found on the floor under the sink to the SERI testing laboratory for comparison with the DNA results for Melanson.

Returning to the issue of chain of custody, Wilensky asked Winegar one question: had he experienced any difficulties locating the pieces of evidence he had ultimately delivered for testing? He responded he had not.

DR. ANTHONY JAY CHAPMAN

Gero next called Dr. Anthony Chapman, a forensic pathologist, for the purpose of establishing the cause of Anita Andrews's death, a critical element of proof in every murder trial. Gero began by asking a series of questions about Dr. Chapman's education, training and more than forty years of experience in forensic pathology. Based on Dr. Chapman's responses, the judge ruled that he qualified as an expert witness, which opened the door to Gero's being able to use the doctor's testimony to educate the jury on accepted forensic standards and practices.

Gero first asked him to explain what an autopsy was.

"An autopsy," Chapman explained, "is a systematic external and internal examination of the body after death, giving consideration to the findings at the scene of death. The primary purpose of an autopsy is to determine the cause and manner of death."

Gero asked if he had reviewed the results of the autopsy performed on Anita Andrews in 1974 by Dr. David Clary. Chapman testified he had reviewed Dr. Clary's report, the autopsy photographs and the investigative reports of the police department.

"After reviewing these reports, had you formed an opinion as to the cause of death in this case?"

"Yes," Chapman answered. "In my opinion, the murderer had stabbed Anita Andrews as many as thirteen times, possibly with the screwdriver found in the bar. The nature of the injuries made it impossible for them to have been inflicted in an accidental or suicidal manner. The only reasonable conclusion was that this death was the result of homicidal violence."

"What about the time of death?" Gero asked.

"No one can accurately pinpoint the time of death," Chapman testified, adding that if information not contained in the original autopsy report had been available, he might have been able to establish a tighter window for the time of death. "That information would be the extent of lividity and rigor mortis."

On cross-examination, Wilensky went straight to the time of death issue. "Doctor, if you *had* had more information, such as extent of lividity, would it have been possible to more accurately estimate time of death?"

"Possibly. There are two major categories that assist in determining time of death. One is development of stiffening of the body that occurs after death, which is called rigor mortis. Lividity is the other category. This is the settling of the blood in the body that occurs after death. It appears as purplish discoloration and then, up to several hours after death, it bleaches out. Neither rigor mortis nor lividity was documented in the autopsy or police investigative reports, so a time-of-death window could not be established. However, I estimated the time of death to be between the hours of midnight and 5:00 a.m."

"Was there any evidence of sexual assault?" Wilensky asked.

"There was no sperm or other fluids," Chapman testified. "And there was no bruising or tearing of the vagina."

24

DNA EVIDENCE

SEPTEMBER 22 AND 23, 2011

CRIMINALIST MICHELLE TERRA

Gero then called criminalist Michelle Terra to the witness stand. Guided by Gero's questioning, Terra testified that she held a bachelor of science degree in molecular biology, with minors in chemistry and photography, from California State University in Sacramento, and she was employed as a senior criminalist and CODIS (Combined DNA Index System, the database where all the millions of DNA profiles are stored) administrator with the California Department of Justice. She also had specialized training with the interpretation of analysis results.

Terra testified that she had been with the Department of Justice for approximately fourteen years and had previously qualified numerous times as an expert witness in forensic DNA analysis and serological (blood) analysis. Based on this testimony, the judge ruled that Terra qualified as an expert witness in forensic DNA analysis and serological analysis. Wilensky did not object.

Gero resumed his questioning by asking Terra to explain how DNA analysis can be used to differentiate one person from another. Terra explained DNA coding and defined the terms *locus* and *loci*. She said loci is the plural of locus, and Gero asked her to orient the jury to the terms she was using. Terra explained that human DNA contains around three billion base pairs (letters) that are separated into twenty-three chromosomes. A genetic locus is the exact location of a gene or genetic marker. This location tells you which chromosome the marker is on as well as exactly where on the chromosome to find it. The locus is similar to an address.

Gero asked, "Is DNA stable over time?"

"Yes," Terra responded, "DNA is stable over time. There are things that can deteriorate DNA over time, but it's not going to morph into somebody else's DNA." She then added, "A person's DNA profile derived from their saliva or blood or semen will always be the same for that person."

Gero asked, "If you had sweat on your hands or forehead and wiped it off with a towel, would that DNA be contained in the sweat?"

"Yes."

"Could it be transferred to a towel?"

"Yes."

"What about DNA in your saliva, could that be transferred to a cigarette?"

"Yes," Terra stated.

Gero then asked if Terra recalled what items she had received from Napa police officer Pete Jerich.

"Yes," she responded, "I do recall those items. I received, in a sealed condition, a blood-soaked terrycloth towel; another towel that had been found on the floor under the sink by the bar; a white towel found at the crotch area of the victim's body; fingernail clippings from the left and right hands of the victim; and hair samples from the victim and from suspect Liston Beal, who had been at the bar earlier that evening. However," Terra continued, "Liston Beal's DNA profile did not match that found on any of the items from the crime scene."

She went on to explain that she had sent the bar towel found on the floor under the bar sink, a reference sample and a control sample to the Serological Research Institute on behalf of the Napa Police Department. She further testified that she received additional items of evidence from the Department of Justice in Sacramento, which included the screwdriver, the cigarette butt, a fragment of glass and a blood sample.

Gero then turned to the results of her tests. Terra testified that she was able to obtain a partial DNA profile from the screwdriver, but it was insufficient for interpretation. The same was true of the towel under the bar sink; the partial DNA profile was insufficient to interpret the test results.

"What about the cigarette butt?"

"I detected a full fifteen DNA locus [specific location] profile from the cigarette butt from an unknown male and I compared that result to DNA from both Liston Beal and Anita Andrews. Both were excluded, so I uploaded the DNA profile of that unknown male to the CODIS DNA database to see if I could find a match."

"Did you find a match from the CODIS database?"

"Yes, I did," Terra answered.

"Of the fifteen loci, how many were matched?"

"All fifteen matched."

Terra went on to explain that the CODIS database is used by local, state and national forensic laboratories. Before the laboratory that determined the match releases a name, its criminalists do their own research and verification. The identification of the unknown male in the bar on the night of the murder was not released to Terra until approximately one month later.

"And what was the name they released to you?" Gero asked.

"The name was Roy Melanson."

Terra then testified that she immediately telephoned Detective Winegar to tell him there was a person of interest in the Anita Andrews murder case. She used *person of interest* until it could be further confirmed that the identified person's profile actually matched the evidence. To do this, she requested a new reference sample from the identified person. "I received those samples of Roy Melanson's DNA from Detective Winegar on December 7, 2009. Those samples were in the form of two buccal reference swabs, along with a blood sample."

"After you compared the buccal swab DNA from Roy Melanson with DNA from the cigarette butt found at the crime scene, what was the result?"

Terra answered, "I determined that the DNA profile from the cigarette butt was the same as the DNA profile from Roy Melanson."

"Did they match on all fifteen locations?"

"Yes, they did," Terra testified.

"How rare is that match?"

"Extremely rare. This evidence profile from the cigarette butt is estimated to occur among unrelated individuals in approximately 1 in 570 quintillion African Americans, 1 in 8.8 quintillion Caucasians and 1 in 170 quintillion Hispanics. This provided strong evidence that Roy Melanson was the source of the DNA on the cigarette butt."

"What exactly is a quintillion?" Gero asked.

"A quintillion," Terra answered, "is the number followed by eighteen zeroes."

Gero then asked what additional evidence Terra received from Detective Winegar on January 29, 2010.

Terra answered, "A green soft drink bottle from the bar stockroom; hairs from the soft drink bottle; the terry cloth towel found on the floor under the bar sink; debris from the terry cloth towel; hair from the stockroom door; hair from the floor of the bar; Anita Andrews's blouse, brassiere and additional clothing, including orange checkered pants, nylon pantyhose, a girdle and underpants; fingernail clippings from Anita Andrews's right and left hands; head and pubic hair from Anita Andrews; a broken glass bottleneck; and seventy-eight microscope slides of hairs, fibers and debris."

She testified that she had examined a total of approximately one hundred items of evidence collected at the crime scene, noting that in a murder case she typically looks at three items. "The policy of the DOJ in a murder case is to examine three items per person, but I examined one hundred items and extracted a total of fifty-six different samples for DNA analysis. Four DNA profiles were developed from these items: these were profiles of Liston Beal, Anita Andrews, Roy Melanson and even my own profile because DNA gets transferred to an item when you're testing it."

"So," Gero queried, "besides yourself and Liston Beal, only Roy Melanson's and Anita Andrews's DNA profiles were found?"

"That is correct."

During cross-examination, defense attorney Wilensky zeroed in on the DNA profile issue. "In order to say you've got a DNA profile match, if you have one donor and you're comparing it to a DNA sample, you would say a fifteen-loci match is a match?"

"Correct," Terra responded. "They are also called location markers."

"Nothing will change that?"

"Right."

Wilensky then turned to the issue of contamination. "In this case you had some contamination issues, correct?"

"I did. Laboratory contamination refers to other DNA that somehow gets in the sample. For instance, the person running the test has their own DNA. If they sneeze or a few skin cells drop into the tube, the analysis could be picking up the DNA 'fingerprint' of the tester rather than the DNA from the sample. When laboratory contamination occurs, it must be recorded. It must also be documented as to how the contamination was dealt with or corrected. If contamination is not recorded, or is improperly recorded, that results in data contamination."

"That was when you tested the bra?"

"Yes."

"And the nylons?"

"Yes."

"And the fingernails?"

"Yes."

Wilensky then changed direction. "How long did you work on this case?" she asked.

"I started in 2004, so it's been approximately seven years off and on."

"Would you say this was a case you were very interested in?"

"Yes. We were looking to do the work to try to include or exclude the suspect so that we could move on to other cases."

Wilensky continued. "When you get a case, is it your job to try to solve a crime or is it your job just to analyze the evidence and turn over your findings?"

"Both," Terra answered. "We look for evidence to support or refute the crime that's been committed. Ultimately, we want to develop evidence that holds the person responsible for the crime accountable."

"It's fair to say that in this case you worked pretty hard to try to find evidence to connect Mr. Melanson to the homicide, is that correct?"

"I worked pretty hard to connect the evidence to whoever was responsible."

Wilensky then asked, "In all the DNA evidence that you developed, you were not able to link Mr. Melanson to the homicide, were you?"

Terra answered, "I did not detect any male DNA on any of the additional items tested."

After Wilensky was finished with her questions, Gero decided to conduct redirect examination. "Do you have any vested interest in this case?" he asked Terra.

"No," Terra replied.

"Had you ever heard of Roy Melanson before you got the DNA match notice from CODIS?"

"No."

"When you do find contamination, do you throw out those results?"

"The contamination is evaluated to determine if it is serious or not, or if it would affect the results."

"Was there any contamination of the DNA sample taken from the cigarette butt?" Gero asked.

"No, there was not."

"Did any of the questions that defense counsel just asked you on cross-examination about contamination change your conclusion that the DNA profile on the cigarette butt matches the DNA profile of Roy Melanson?"

"No. That does not change my test results or my conclusion."

With that, Gero concluded his redirect examination.

Senior Criminalist Deanna Kacer

The trial resumed the next morning with Gero calling to the witness stand Deanna Kacer, a senior criminalist with the Department of Justice Sacramento crime laboratory. Once the court recognized her as an expert witness in forensic DNA analysis, Kacer testified that she had been asked to develop a Y-STR (gender chromosome) DNA profile for Roy Melanson for comparison with evidence previously typed by SERI in Richmond, California.

She explained that the Y stands for the Y chromosome. This means that the scientist looked only for DNA regions from the Y chromosome. The Y chromosome was used because it makes it impossible to have contamination from female DNA, as females do not have Y chromosomes. Since only men have the Y chromosome, this test automatically cuts the suspect pool in half. The number in front of the Y-STR (Short Tandem Repeat) is a locus number; for example, seventeen locus stands for the number of locations on the Y chromosome that are observed in this test. There were seventeen regions that are part of this test. The reason they do this type of testing instead of just sequencing all the DNA is that 99.9 percent of human DNA is identical. By doing these tests, a scientist can focus just on the regions that are most likely to be different between individuals.

Kacer testified that, in this case, "the seventeen-locus Y-STR DNA, male DNA haplotype was detected from the reference sample taken from Roy Melanson. I sent those results to the DOJ Central Valley lab, the Napa Police Department, the Napa District Attorney's Office, and to SERI for comparison with previous test results."

Wilensky's cross-examination was once again brief, focusing on the question of possible instances of evidence contamination. It appeared that the general thrust of her questioning was to create doubt regarding the overall reliability of the tests being described by the prosecution's witnesses.

At the conclusion of Wilensky's cross-examination, Gero once again rose for redirect questioning. In a series of questions, he established that there was no evidence of any contamination having occurred during testing at the DOJ Sacramento laboratory.

Forensic Serologist Gary Harmor

Gero's next witness was forensic serologist Gary Harmor, assistant lab director with the Serological Research Institute, an accredited research laboratory engaged in identification of blood, semen, saliva and other body fluids. For the Andrews homicide investigation, Harmor said he performed tests for male DNA on the bloodstained bar towel received from DOJ criminalist Michelle Terra in 2006 and could develop only a partial DNA profile. That was sufficient to rule out Liston Beal as a suspect, but Harmor could not identify the male DNA donor. However, Harmor testified that, based on the DNA profile of Roy Melanson provided by Deanna Kacer of the DOJ, "Roy Melanson could be the source of the male DNA detected on the bloodstained bar towel."

Harmor went on to testify that his further analysis confirmed that the Y-STR profile was consistent with that of Roy Melanson.

On cross-examination, Wilensky flatly stated that inspection by the FBI and the American Society of Crime Lab Directors Lab Accreditation Board had revealed possible irregularities in the SERI laboratory documentation relating to contamination.

Harmor responded, "That's not quite true. We did document in the case folder when there was any evidence of contamination. What we hadn't been doing, which became the standard in July 2009, was compiling a record of contamination events or mislabeled samples."

Wilensky continued her line of questioning. "Between the beginning of 2008 and the time you completed your analysis in this case, there was rampant contamination in the lab, was there not?"

Harmor replied, "There had been isolated contamination events through 2009, but in July 2010 we shut down DNA extractions until we isolated the contamination source."

Gero's redirect examination focused on this contamination issue. "Did your lab pass the subsequent audits or inspections by the FBI and the American Society of Crime Lab Directors Lab Accreditation Board?"

"Yes," Harmor testified.

"And did the 2006 and 2010 lab results that you reported comply with quality assurance standards?"

"Yes, they did."

On recross-examination, Wilensky zeroed in on the contamination issue. "The fact remains that you don't know that those DNA markers came from one person?"

"That's correct," Harmor conceded. "That was an assumption on my part."

25

THE JURY VISITS THE MURDER SCENE AT FAGIANI'S BAR

SEPTEMBER 23, 2011

P rior to the beginning of the trial, one of Gero's pretrial motions was to allow the jury to visit the scene of the crime. Gero argued that photographs could not adequately convey the layout of the bar and how small the storage room is. Moreover, Gero argued that the cocktail lounge had largely the same layout as it did in 1974, and any differences could be explained to the jury during the visit. Finally, Gero argued that the lounge was one block from the courthouse and would require minimal disruption of the trial. Wilensky voiced an objection that any visit must be done under adequate supervision by the court. She explained there is an inherent danger in moving the jury as a group to a different location because they could start conversations among themselves or with other people once they are not in the more controlled setting of a courtroom. The concern regarding jurors mingling and talking with others is that they could start forming or expressing opinions about the case, based on such conversations. These conversations are not part of the trial evidence that can be legally considered by the jury.

Such a request is unusual for a thirty-seven-year-old case. After the passage of time, the scene of the crime may not even exist or may be substantially changed. In his ruling, the judge reasoned that the scene had been largely preserved and it might be helpful to the jury to see the layout of the lounge in person as opposed to photographs. This, coupled with the convenience of the location of the bar to the courthouse, persuaded the judge to allow the jury to visit the scene. However, the judge agreed with

Wilensky that the visit must be under strict conditions. The judge would instruct the bailiff to keep the jurors together in a group and allow no one to speak to them, nor allow them to speak to one another about any subject connected with the trial.

The time had arrived for the jury to visit the crime scene.

The judge informed the jury they would be traveling to the scene at the conclusion of Harmor's testimony. He explained the rules of such a visit. They would all walk across the street from the courthouse to Fagiani's Cocktail Lounge. They were not to speak or pose any questions except when the judge told them they could. The judge also told the jury they could expect to see original photographs of the bar for comparison to its present condition. The new owner, Steve Hasty, would explain what had changed since he became the owner in 2007. And the attorneys would be permitted to ask questions of Hasty or answer questions from the jurors.

The visit included the twelve jurors and the three alternate jurors, the judge, three attorneys (Gero, his colleague Scott Young and Wilensky), three bailiffs, the court reporter, court clerks and several police investigators. Also present was a reporter from the *Napa Valley Register*. All members of this group would walk over at the same time, escorted by the bailiffs. The defendant, Roy Melanson, waived his right to be personally present for the visit and was returned to the jail.

After a brief recess, the judge led the jury out of the courtroom and across the street to the crime scene. The rest of the group followed quietly. Steve Hasty had already unlocked the door. Some of the bailiffs went in first, and the judge and jurors and other members of the group filed in behind them.

The room in which the jurors and the entourage of court officials found themselves was not exactly the same as the one in which witnesses had testified to having seen the victim and the accused regarding each other across the bar more than three decades earlier. Fagiani's had stood frozen in time, unused and undisturbed, until Anita's sister, Muriel, sold the property to Steve Hasty in 2007. Hasty, however, did not begin an ambitious remodel of the property until a few months before the trial. His goal was to repurpose the building as a restaurant.

When the jury visited, the work had been underway for several months. Many of the interior walls had been torn down, and the stockroom where Anita's body had been found was gone. However, one element of the original Fagiani's had been carefully preserved: the long bar, where the original barstools still stood in the exact positions they had been found by police the morning after the murder.

The jurors were allowed to walk along the bar and observe the stool, pulled slightly out, where David Luce testified he and his two friends saw Melanson so many years ago. The remainder of the ground floor was in disarray, with items strewn about due to the remodeling. Hasty was also renovating the second-floor offices.

Once the jury had had the opportunity to take in the scene, prosecutor Gero obtained the judge's permission to pass around enlarged photographs of the bar as it had been in 1974.

The *Napa Valley Register* reporter described the scene: "Jurors could be seen standing in the middle of the room and stepping behind the old, dusty mahogany bar where Anita Andrews had once stood serving customers who had been coming to her family's establishment since the 1940's. Missing were the [original] inside walls, including those of the stockroom where Andrews' sister, Muriel Fagiani, had discovered Anita's body on the morning of July 11, 1974."

Steve Hasty explained the changes he had made but stated that the bar and the barstools were the same as they were in 1974, as were the sink and faucets behind the bar. "Everything back there is original," he said.

Some of the jurors had questions. One asked what was underneath the building.

"A small basement," Hasty explained.

Gero asked Hasty about the lighting underneath the bar.

"There were 12 by 12 squares that had little light bulbs and some blue chip-type glass in them that provided very dim lighting. And these walls had say, two, maybe three, half-sconces, and there were three stuffed deer heads."

"Were the rear windows operable?" Gero continued.

"They were operable originally, yes."

A juror asked one last question. "Did you come in here in the seventies and were you able to see the layout?"

Hasty answered, "No."

This concluded the visit to the homicide scene, and the group returned to the courthouse.

By now it was after 3:00 p.m. on a Friday afternoon, and the judge decided it would be better to adjourn for the day, rather than call the next witness. He reminded the jury of the importance of not discussing the trial or reading any press accounts and then dismissed them for the weekend.

Once the last juror had filed out, Gero asked to make a comment off the record. "In preparation for this trial I have been to the old bar several times, and I have to tell you, every time I go in there it feels eerie knowing what happened there."

After a thoughtful pause, Wilensky responded, "It definitely felt strange for me, too."

Gero added, "I'm guessing the jurors must have had strange feelings about being where such a brutal murder took place decades ago. I'll bet it was an eerie atmosphere for everyone."

The attorneys then turned their attention to the business of the trial, saying they now believed the case would be submitted to the jury for deliberation the following week.

With that, the judge adjourned the trial until Monday morning.

26

TESTIMONY CONTINUES

SEPTEMBER 26, 2011

WITNESS JOE SILVA

The trial resumed Monday morning with prosecuting attorney Gero calling Joe Silva as a witness.

Silva was raised in Napa and worked as an electrician at Mare Island Naval Shipyard in Vallejo. Silva testified he had known Anita Andrews since 1969 or 1970, when he moved into the front unit apartment in an old Victorian house and Anita was living in the back unit. He saw her two or three times a week and described her as "very nice, warm, friendly, easy to talk to. I'd say dependable, just an ordinary…a good person, a swell person."

In his questioning, Gero established that Silva and Anita Andrews had never had a romantic relationship.

Sometime in 1972 or 1973, Silva testified, the house in which their apartments were located was sold, and they both had to move. Silva bought a house and Anita moved to an apartment on Soscol Avenue, but they remained friends. Silva said he knew Anita worked at the Napa State Hospital during the day and at Fagiani's bar in the evenings every day except Sunday. He testified he visited Anita at Fagiani's probably three or four times a week and usually found the bar sparsely populated, with never more than four people there at any one time.

Gero then asked if he knew the car Anita drove. Silva said it was a beige 1967 Cadillac. He identified the vehicle in a photograph Gero showed him and stated that he was familiar with Anita's custom of parking her Cadillac in front of the bar. After her murder, Silva testified he and a friend searched for the car in Napa and San Francisco, including at the international airport. For weeks after the murder, Silva said he was vigilant, hoping to spot the Cadillac while driving around town. He never saw the car again.

When asked if he knew whether Anita had a boyfriend at the time she was killed, Silva responded she did not. On cross-examination, Wilensky asked if Silva had ever gone to the bar at closing time. "No, never," he replied.

"Were you supposed to see Anita the night before she was killed?"

Silva initially replied he didn't remember.

Wilensky then cited a September 2010 conversation Silva had with Investigator Leslie Severe in which he told Severe that the night before Anita was killed he had asked her out to dinner, and she had accepted. However, she later called him back and asked for a rain check.

"Was this out of the ordinary for Anita?"

"Yes, it was," Silva said, "because Anita had never canceled plans before."

On redirect examination, Gero asked Silva about an interview a few days after the murder during which Silva told Lieutenants Bailey and Jarecki that two days before Anita was killed, on July 8, 1974, he had called Fagiani's at approximately 4:30 p.m. and invited Anita to dinner when she closed the bar at 8:00 p.m. However, at 8:00 p.m. Anita had called Silva back and asked for a rain check.

Silva said this was true.

On recross-examination, Wilensky asked if Anita had ever called him from the bar and asked him to pretend to be her boyfriend.

Silva said that was true, but it had happened months before the murder. "Anita asked me to pretend to be her boyfriend because there was a creep in the bar. I was to call her back and pretend I was her boyfriend because she wanted him out of there."

"How many times did that happen?" Wilensky asked.

Silva answered, "Once."

Witness Donna Andrews Hawkins

Gero's next witness was Donna Hawkins, Anita Andrews's younger daughter. Donna testified that her father was Mike Andrews and that he and her mother had separated soon after she was born. Donna and her older sister, Diana, had been raised by their mother, and Donna also had a close relationship with her aunt, Muriel Fagiani.

Donna testified that her mother was a hard worker, employed as a secretary at Napa State Hospital and cared for her two daughters. She said her father never contributed child support, so her mother had always worked. Weekdays she worked from 8:00 a.m. to 4:00 p.m. and was home by 4:30 p.m. She would then go to the bar around 5:00 p.m. and keep it open for about four hours. Her mother worked at the bar every day except Sunday, when the bar was closed.

"Aunt Muriel also worked at the bar," Donna testified, "but she didn't work as much because she wasn't real good with people, didn't like to converse back and forth." Donna further stated that her mother "was very picky about our house. We had to have it clean and neat all the time." Also, Donna added, "She never wore pants unless she was inside the house and nobody saw her. But when she went out and about she always had on nice clothes and matching shoes. She always had jewelry; she always wore a nice necklace and earrings. She was never sloppy."

Gero asked if she remembered when her mother was killed. "Yes," Donna replied. "I was twenty-three years old at the time." She testified the last time she saw her mother alive was approximately a week before her murder, when Anita had visited Donna in Walnut Creek, where Donna was living at the time.

"Was anything troubling your mother at the time?"

"Yes," Donna replied. "There was a gentleman that had bothered her. He had run her phone bill up to $400, and she had his tools in the trunk of her car so that he would have to pay her back." Otherwise, Donna testified, her mother had been in good spirits.

Gero then established Donna's familiarity with the layout of Fagiani's bar. Donna testified she had been in the office upstairs and had seen a safe located there.

"Are you familiar with your mother's signature?"

"Yes, because I used to do it when I was a kid at school, so I know how she wrote it. I forged her signature on notes when I wanted to cut school."

Gero presented a copy of a gas receipt and asked Donna if she had ever seen that signature before.

"No," she testified. "That's not her signature. She did not write like that."

On cross-examination, Wilensky asked about the man who had run up her mother's phone bill. "When you saw your mom about a week before she was killed, there was a man she was worried about?"

"Yes, but she wasn't worried. She was mad because he owed her money and she wanted him to pay the money for the phone bill."

"Did your mother take his tools?"

"Yes. She had them in the trunk of her car."

DETECTIVE DON WINEGAR

A prosecution case is made up of numerous bits of information elicited from a stream of witnesses. To assist the jury to better understand the case, prosecutors will often endeavor to control the order in which information is presented. So it was that Gero's next witness was Detective Winegar, who was recalled to provide additional direct testimony. In his previous testimony, Winegar had described collection of DNA from Melanson. Now Gero sought to elicit further aspects of Winegar's investigation.

Winegar testified that on November 24, 2009, he directed an investigator at the prison to obtain Melanson's fingerprints and personally observed the process. The investigator then gave the fingerprint sheet to Winegar, who labeled it, transported it back to Napa and turned it over to Napa Police Department forensic technician Janet Lipsey.

Gero then asked, "On that same day, November 24, 2009, did you also take a handwriting sample from Mr. Melanson?"

"Yes. I watched Mr. Melanson write out the sample, which I took back to the Napa Police Department and booked into evidence. Then on January 29, 2010, I took that handwriting sample, along with a copy of the credit card gasoline purchase receipt to Sean Espley at the Department of Justice in Sacramento." Winegar went on to explain that Espley later requested additional handwriting samples from Melanson, so he returned to Colorado on October 1, 2010, and obtained them.

Gero asked if Winegar had attempted to locate witnesses involved in the original Napa Police Department investigation. Winegar responded that he found this to be one of the hardest parts of his job. "It was a thirty-seven-year-old case, and that was the most challenging part for me. Most of the witnesses, or a lot of the witnesses, and even police officers, were deceased."

"How many witnesses did you identify?" Gero inquired.

"Approximately...probably around 150. That's counting officers, too." He added that he had spent approximately two thousand hours investigating this case.

"Did you do a background investigation on Roy Melanson?"

"I did," Winegar said. "I traveled to three different states and talked to several members of Melanson's family as well as to law enforcement personnel."

"Did any witnesses see a photo lineup you had prepared?"

"Yes. I showed David Luce a photo lineup. After forty or forty-five seconds, Luce picked out photo number six as the person he had seen in the bar on the night of the murder. Photo number six was Roy Melanson."

"Why did Luce believe that photo number six was the person he saw in the bar that night?"

"Luce said it was the eyes he recalled the most."

Gero again directed Winegar's attention to his interview with Melanson on November 30, 2009. "What was Mr. Melanson's demeanor when you met with him?"

"Melanson was cooperative at first, and polite," Winegar stated. "But the more the conversation centered around Napa and the murder case, Melanson's demeanor changed. He just became tighter. And eventually, Melanson ended the interview."

At this point, the recorded interview between Winegar and Melanson was presented to the jury. The jury showed no perceptible reaction to watching the interview on video.

During cross-examination, Wilensky delved into Winegar's preparation of his photo lineup, pointing out that the photos were not from the same period and that Melanson's photo stood out as being from the 1970s. However, Winegar maintained he had very carefully selected and prepared the six-picture photo lineup to make the subjects look as similar as possible, using photographs of other males similar in age, race and facial hair.

Wilensky continued pressing him on the matter. "The shirt Melanson was wearing in the subject photo was a 1970s plaid collared shirt with the collar sticking out, which dated his picture to the 1970s. Because Melanson was the only person in the line-up wearing 1970s style clothes, this suggests the photo lineup was unfair."

To this Winegar responded, "That's the way you describe it. I just saw a shirt."

Wilensky then asked about a rum bottle that had been fingerprinted. "Do you know why Detective Bailey went back to the bar to retrieve that rum bottle?"

"Yes," Winegar said. "Detective Bailey spoke to someone who was in the bar that evening who had observed a person he didn't know sitting at the bar where the ashtray and cigarette butt had been found. That person had assisted the victim in opening a bottle, the rum bottle, and pouring a drink."

On redirect examination, Gero returned to the photo lineup, asking why Winegar hadn't used old photographs to create the photo lineup.

"I could not find similar photos of the suspect that would match the photo lineup I was trying to make," Winegar testified.

"Did you find a bunch of people that looked similar to Mr. Melanson?"

"No," Winegar said. "I did not."

Forensic Document Analyst Sean Espley

Gero's next witness was Sean Espley, the forensic document examiner whom Detective Winegar had mentioned in his testimony. After the judge qualified Espley as an expert in his field, Gero asked about his examination of a gas receipt Winegar had submitted to Espley in January 2010.

Espley testified that he had compared the copy of the gas receipt provided by the credit card company to a handwriting sample from Roy Melanson, looking for similarities or dissimilarities in certain features of the writing. He examined how specific letters were formed, such as whether the crossing on a capital T was from left to right or right to left, or whether a capital O was made in a clockwise or counterclockwise fashion. He also studied the spacing between letters, height relationships between letters, the beginning and ending strokes of letters or words and how the writer adheres to the baseline when he signs his name (whether the signature goes along the baseline or cuts through the baseline, uphill or downhill).

"And what were the results of your initial examination?" Gero asked.

"The biggest challenge was the gas receipt," Espley said. "It was a poor copy, so many features of the signature could not be examined and compared to the writing sample from Mr. Melanson. There were a few generic similarities, by which I mean pictorial resemblances of letter forms and how a particular letter starts and ends, but the comparison was basically inconclusive. Beyond those similarities, the rest of the gas receipt signature was somewhat illegible, partly because it was a bad copy and partly because it was just a scribble and not a signature. Mr. Melanson could be neither identified nor eliminated as the author of the Anita Andrews signature on the gas receipt."

On cross-examination, Wilensky asked whether Espley would have been able to do a proper comparison with an original gas receipt rather than a poor copy.

"Yes," he said. "With original letters I could have looked at a lot more things within the signature itself."

"Given what you were provided, two items to compare, your conclusion was that you could not exclude Mr. Melanson?"

"That is correct."

"And you also cannot identify the signature source as Mr. Melanson?"

"That is correct."

"So you don't know?" Wilensky pursued.

"No, I don't know," Espley said. "My examination was inconclusive."

Forensic Specialist Janet Lipsey

Continuing his focus on forensic evidence analysis, Gero's next witness was forensic specialist Janet Lipsey. She testified that she had worked for the Napa Police Department for forty years, thirty-four of those as a specialist in forensic evidence collection, processing, analysis, forensic photography and fingerprint identification.

Gero asked her to explain to the jury how fingerprints are compared, and she described the process. "When you touch surfaces, most of the impressions you leave behind are not visible and need to be developed. These are called latent prints."

Lipsey explained that to develop latent prints for comparison purposes, she would use a finger brush and black fingerprint powder to dust the surface of an object. As the dust adhered to the oils that composed the print, the print would "develop" so she could see it. Then she could photograph the print or lift it with clear fingerprint tape and place it on a clean white card to preserve the print for later comparison.

"I can then make a comparison between the latent print and a known inked print. I look for ridge characteristics, called points of identification."

Gero asked, "How many points of comparison are necessary in order to render an identification?"

"The FBI uses a minimum of eight points of comparison to make an identification. I am much more comfortable with nine or ten."

"Did you compare submitted fingerprints collected from Fagiani's bar in the Anita Andrews homicide case?"

"Yes," she answered. "In 2009 and 2010 Detective Winegar asked me to compare additional prints submitted in the Andrews case with those booked as evidence in 1974."

Napa Police Department evidence technician Janet Lipsey. *Courtesy of the Napa Police Historical Society.*

"And the results?"

"I had mixed results," Lipsey said. "I was able to match some points of comparison, but I was unable to match others. I looked at the screwdriver that was booked into evidence and reported that no prints were developed from it. The fingerprints on a broken green bottle were not sufficiently detailed to determine a match. I also looked at the shoe prints that were booked into evidence, but I was unable to make any identification."

Gero then asked about Budweiser bottles found in a case behind the bar. Lipsey testified that she was able to determine fingerprint matches on those bottles. "I also looked at a Brugal rum bottle and found matches with latent fingerprints."

Gero then produced an ashtray collected from the bar and asked whether she had made any comparisons of fingerprints found on the rum bottle or the ashtray.

Lipsey responded that she had compared the fingerprints taken from Roy Melanson submitted by Detective Winegar to the ones obtained from evidence in 1974. "They came from the same person. In comparing those fingerprints from the crime scene with the prints from Roy Melanson, I found a match on three beer bottles. The prints were made by Roy Melanson. I also found several prints from Melanson on the rum bottle. The total number of matches was thirteen, nine matches on the Budweiser bottles and four matches on the rum bottle. There were no dissimilarities."

On cross-examination, Wilensky asked whether there were any prints on the beer bottles that did not match Melanson's.

"Yes," Lipsey said. "I did identify the fingerprints of Anita Andrews."

"Were there any other prints besides those of Mr. Melanson and Anita Andrews?"

Lipsey replied that she thought there were, but she did not know to whom those prints belonged.

"Did you say to anybody, 'I have a good print here, and it's not Mr. Melanson's'?"

"Yes. I did have latent prints from the Budweiser bottles that were not Mr. Melanson's, and I submitted those prints to the Department of Justice."

"At the Department of Justice," Wilensky inquired, "what happened to the latent prints that did not match Melanson's?"

Lipsey replied that she didn't know. "I was told that DOJ would run them through California's system at the DOJ as well as the Western Identification Network [a database for identifying fingerprints for states outside California], but I don't know if that was ever done."

At this point it became apparent that Wilensky was trying to raise doubt as to the thoroughness of Lipsey's fingerprint identification. On redirect examination, Gero's only question to Lipsey was whether she had examined *all* of the fingerprints that she detected on the items of evidence submitted to her by investigators.

"Yes," Lipsey testified. "I did."

Forensic DNA Consultant Norah Rudin

A jury trial is somewhat like a play unfolding before the jurors in acts and scenes. The first act is the opening statements by the attorneys, the second act is the presentation of the prosecution's witnesses and the third act is the presentation of the defense witnesses. The last act is the closing arguments of the attorneys. However, exceptions occasionally arise, as was the case with the testimony of forensic DNA consultant Norah Rudin. Because of her tight schedule and limited availability, she was the next witness called, even though she was a defense witness appearing in the midst of the prosecution's case.

As a defense witness, Rudin was first examined by defense attorney Wilensky, who began by asking about her credentials and experience. This included twenty years working as a private forensic DNA consultant. Upon being recognized by the judge as an expert in her field, Rudin went on to explain that such consultants normally review the data, notes and reports generated by laboratories conducting forensic analyses to determine whether the consultant agrees with the laboratory's conclusions.

In the Andrews homicide case, Rudin testified she reviewed all the laboratory notes, including those from the Serological Research Institute, the audit reports of independent state agencies conducting annual reviews of SERI and raw data generated in the testing process. She then conducted her own independent analysis of all this information. Wilensky asked if she found anything that, in her expert opinion, was significant in her independent analysis.

"Yes," Rudin answered. "The state auditors conducting annual audits of SERI found quite a few issues, including two issues that relate to this case in particular. One had to do with data contamination, and the other had to do with the database used to determine frequency of DNA marker occurrence, or the weight of the evidence."

Wilensky directed Rudin's attention to the specific work and testimony of forensic serologist Gary Harmor. "Regarding the DNA profile analysis work of Gary Harmor at SERI, how reliable were Harmor's conclusions?"

Rudin responded, "Harmor's conclusions were based on the assumption that all of the DNA samples came from a single person. And in this case, that's not necessarily a reliable assumption."

Wilensky pursued the matter. "In this case is there anything about the information that you reviewed, that is, the information the SERI laboratory used, that could lead to the assumption that the towel submitted in evidence had only one man's DNA on it?"

"No," Rudin answered. "Mr. Harmor took little cuttings from all around the towel, not from just one place and not from a visible stain. There was nothing that would lead you to believe the DNA was from one person, especially with the type of male chromosomal DNA markers where there's one number for each location. Many men may share partial DNA profiles."

Wilensky then asked Rudin to expand.

"When you have a little sample from here and a little sample from there, you are not at all sure *this* allele, which is a gene location marker, and *that* allele are from the same person."

"Is there anything about the DNA analysis results that indicate the DNA had to come from one person?" Wilensky asked.

"No," Rudin said.

"Mr. Harmor testified that there was a DNA marker that could *not* have belonged to Mr. Melanson. Did you see that as well?"

Rudin responded, "Yes, I did."

"He testified that was a very weak marker?"

"All the profiles were extremely weak," Rudin said. "The markers that could have come from Mr. Melanson were very weak. And there was more than one weak marker in that DNA profile that could *not* have come from Mr. Melanson. It was weaker, but again, all the markers were weak."

In the prosecution's cross-examination, attorney Gero asked Rudin when she had last performed DNA testing herself.

"Probably in the mid-1990s or so," she stated.

"Has testing changed at all since the mid-1990s?"

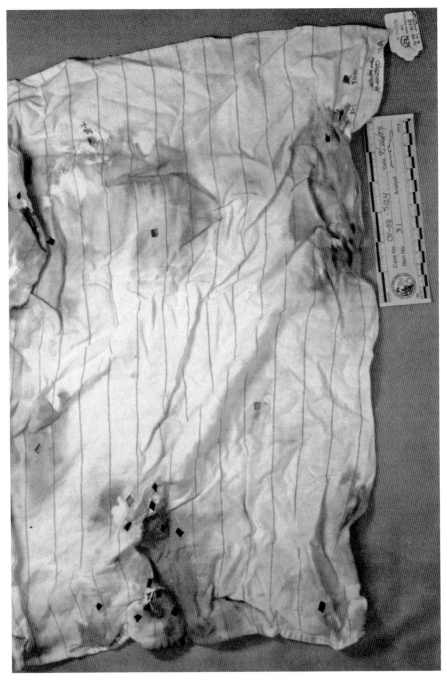

Evidence photo of bloody towel depicting the "cuttings" taken for DNA testing. The DNA evidence was heavily criticized by defense witness Norah Rudin. *Courtesy of the Napa County District Attorney's Office.*

"The basic technology has not changed," Rudin said, "though some new systems have been introduced, for example Y-STR DNA testing, which looks at specific location markers on the Y, or male, chromosome. However, the laboratory procedures are really quite similar."

"But you have not done Y-STR DNA testing?" Gero asked.

"I have reviewed quite a lot of data, but I haven't specifically done Y-STR testing as opposed to standard STR testing."

Gero pressed her. "So, you have not done Y-STR DNA testing before. Is that true or not true?"

"Well, in the laboratory I haven't performed the physical procedures, but as I mentioned I looked at a lot of data."

Gero then asked, "When was Y-STR DNA testing, looking at specific markers on the male chromosome, generally used in the scientific community?"

"Some laboratories were starting to use it around 2005 or 2006," Rudin answered.

"As a consultant, does your work primarily consist of reviewing other people's data, experiments and testing?"

"Yes. I basically do an independent review of data. I get what is called raw data, and I review it independently and come to my own conclusions. Then I compare my conclusions to those in other submitted reports and try to determine whether I agree that the data support their conclusions."

Gero then turned to the audit issues performed by state auditors regarding SERI that Rudin had raised. "You said it was common to find laboratory auditors' issues, but you believed that, in this particular case, there were a lot of them."

"Yes. There were more auditing issues than I normally see."

"But the SERI lab ended up passing their subsequent audit, true?"

"Yes, they did," Rudin conceded.

"And," Gero continued, "the SERI lab has been continually accredited since 1999?"

"Yes."

"Did the testing done in this case in 2010 comply with the updated standards set in 2009 by the FBI Quality Assurance Standards?"

"Yes, with the exception that SERI was not following protocol regarding databases. But in terms of the other areas I looked at, yes, it did comply."

"You talked about laboratory contamination," Gero continued. "Can you clarify?"

"Yes. There was certainly lab contamination in this case, and that included Y-STR DNA profile analysis."

"All such contamination is documented, right?" Gero inquired.

"Well, actually, the contamination in this case wasn't."

"But the contamination in this case actually *was* documented," Gero stated. "That's how you learned about it. Isn't that true?"

"No," Rudin testified. "I learned about the contamination in two different ways. First, because I actually reviewed it by independently re-analyzing the raw data, as I mentioned. And second, because some of the contamination *was* documented."

"You analyzed the raw DNA database, isn't that true?"

"Yes," Rudin said.

"And the frequency of occurrence of Mr. Melanson's DNA profile would be observed once in 11,393 males, isn't that true?"

"Yes," Rudin replied, "but with a caveat. It was actually the evidence DNA profile, not Mr. Melanson's DNA sample profile, and there was actually an error in Mr. Harmor's report. The fewer the gene markers found in the evidence DNA profile, the more males could possibly have contributed to it."

Gero persisted. "So, the DNA gene marker in the evidence DNA profile would be observed in 1 out of 11,393 males?"

"No. Ultimately, the frequency of observed DNA gene marker identification was 1 out of 3,846."

"The Applied Biosystems database has a profile of 11,393 men in it, does it not?" Gero asked.

"Yes."

"And the DNA profile that matched Roy Melanson's was seen one time in those 11,393 men. So, the rarity of that profile in the population is 0.0088 percent. And the U.S. Y-STR database has 10,925 men in it. So, the evidence DNA profile that was consistent with the actual DNA sample from Roy Melanson was found one time in 10,925 men in that database, correct?"

"Yes, but that is the raw statistic. The corrected statistic is 1 in 3,846."

On redirect examination Wilensky asked, "And the 95 percent confidence rate that Mr. Harmor received from his database was 1 in 3,846, correct?"

"Yes."

"But when you ran the data through the U.S. Y-STR database, you came out with a confidence rate of 1 in 2,981?"

"Yes," Rudin acknowledged.

"Was this strong information?" Wilensky asked.

"No," Rudin stated. "It was still a partial DNA profile, and it was an extremely weak profile."

"There was DNA present that could *not* have belonged to Mr. Melanson, correct?"

"Right. According to Mr. Harmor, there was an extra piece of information that could not have been from Mr. Melanson."

Wilensky returned to the issue of contamination. "Sometime in 2009 the SERI laboratory started keeping a contamination log, as required. Is that correct?"

"Yes," Rudin testified.

"And then they did additional testing in this case?"

"Yes," Rudin said again.

"After the lab had been audited, and it started keeping a log, there was still contamination in this case, correct?"

"Yes."

Wilensky's questioning complete, it was Gero's turn for recross-examination. He addressed the issue of the strength of DNA testing results by asking, "When I asked you about the Y-STR DNA testing database that you liked, I used the 1 in 10,925 frequency of where the partial DNA profile is seen. That means the chance of that profile occurring in the population is very rare. Correct?"

"Right," Rudin testified.

Gero knew that although the DNA on the cigarette butt was incontrovertibly Melanson's, it proved only that he'd been in the bar. Rudin's testimony was critical in linking Melanson to the killing. It was important whether some of the DNA on the bloody towel was his, because that was stronger evidence of his involvement in the killing of Anita Andrews. The towel found under the bar sink had the DNA of both the victim and the defendant on it, placing them together *and* placing the defendant behind the bar.

Apparently concluding that he had done all he could to reinforce the DNA test results in the minds of the jury, Gero told the judge he had no more questions.

NAPA POLICE CAPTAIN ROBERT JARECKI

Gero's next witness was Captain Robert Jarecki, who began his testimony by explaining he had worked for the Napa Police Department for thirty years. After retiring, he worked for fifteen years as an investigator with the Napa District Attorney's Office. At the time of the 1974 Andrews homicide,

Jarecki was a police lieutenant and shared the role of lead investigator on the case with Lieutenant John Bailey.

Moving to the substance of the case, Gero asked Jarecki if he recalled showing David Luce a photo lineup in 1974. Jarecki testified he did not.

During cross-examination, Wilensky handed Jarecki a two-page photo lineup and asked, "Would that be the photo lineup you showed to Mr. Luce?"

Seeing the document apparently refreshed Jarecki's memory because he responded, "In reviewing a report I made in 1974, yes, it is."

Sensing an opportunity to cast doubt on Luce's identification of Melanson, Wilensky asked, "You showed Luce that photo lineup because at the time you

Napa police lieutenant Robert Jarecki. *Courtesy of the Napa Police Historical Society.*

were interested in a Liston Beal, who is photo number 8. Is that correct?"

"Yes. I asked Luce if he recognized anyone in those photos that he had seen at Fagiani's bar on the night of the murder. He said it could be photo number 1 or it could be number 8."

Having now established that Luce had previously identified two other possible suspects, as neither photo number 1 nor 8 was Roy Melanson, Wilensky concluded her cross-examination.

Fearing that Wilensky may have succeeded in casting doubt on Luce's credibility, Gero felt it important to clarify that Luce had picked two people in the first lineup thirty-six years before Melanson's photo appeared in any lineup shown to Luce.

Gero asked Jarecki, "You said Luce indicated he recognized the individual in either photo number 1 or photo number 8. Do you recall that Luce said that the image *closest* to the person he recognized was photo number 1, and photo number 8 was *second-closest*?"

"Yes," Jarecki testified, "I do recall that."

This concluded Gero's questioning of Jarecki.

27

EVIDENCE OF PAST CRIMES

SEPTEMBER 27, 2011

Witness Sandra Sue Arnold Schiller

Gero now shifted from offering evidence relating to the Andrews murder to prior acts committed by Roy Melanson. These acts were the ones in Melanson's history that were the subject of intense argument during the pretrial motions. One of these acts was a prior rape that the judge ruled admissible for the jury's consideration, because it showed Melanson's propensity to commit a sex offense and also his general method of gaining the trust of unsuspecting female victims.

Gero's first witness regarding Melanson's prior behavior was Sandra Sue Arnold Schiller. She began her testimony by explaining that in 1974 she was seventeen years old and living in Bridge City, Texas, under her maiden name of Arnold. She stated she did not know Roy Melanson at that time.

Gero asked, "Do you remember driving to a gas station in Texas on February 20, 1974?"

"Yes," Schiller answered. "I had just dropped my boyfriend off at DuPont, where he worked."

"What happened when you got to the gas station?"

Schiller said, "I pulled in and got out of my car and saw that nobody was there and that there was no gas because of the gas shortage back then. Mr. Melanson pulled in behind me, also looking for gas, I thought. He said he knew of a gas station that he thought *did* have gas and we could go fill our cars up."

"What did Mr. Melanson look like at the time?"

"Um, like an older man," Schiller responded. "He had greasy hair, slicked back. He looked like an old cowboy. He reminded me of my grandpa."

"Do you see him in the courtroom?" Gero asked.

"Yes, I do," Schiller said emphatically, pointing to Melanson. Enunciating clearly, she stated, "He's right there."

"Did Mr. Melanson propose a plan to get gas?"

"Uh, yes," Schiller said. "He said he felt for sure there was a gas station down the road, and he wanted me to follow him just in case he ran out of gas or something went wrong with his truck. And he said if…if he was following me and he pulled over, to pull over and see if he needed help."

"And?" Gero pursued.

"And he had the hood up on his truck and was messing with something underneath and wanted me to get in his truck and try to start it. So, I did. And when I did that, he got in the truck and pushed me down onto the floorboard. And then my nightmare started."

"Before that day, had you ever seen or talked to Mr. Melanson?"

"No."

"What happened when he pushed you down on the floorboard?"

"Uh, he told me not to get up or he'd kill me. He drove his truck and I was down on the floorboard. He took me to this big field. He stopped his truck in that field, and he raped me."

"And when you say 'rape,'" Gero said, "you mean he used force when he had sexual intercourse with you?"

"Yes."

"Did he tie you up at any point?"

"Yes," Schiller said. "It was starting to get dark out. I saw a car pull up way out, you know. It had its lights on, so I started to lay on the horn, seeing if somebody would notice me or see that I was in trouble. I was trying to get away. And that's when he tied me up. He tied me up with my pantyhose and gagged me."

Gero then asked, "At the first location in the field, did he rape you one time or more than one time?"

"Several times," Schiller answered.

"And then did he drive to a second location?"

"Yes. He drove me to an Orange Field garbage dump, and he raped me again."

"Did he ever use anything else besides pantyhose to tie you up?"

"I believe he got some rope out of the back of his truck."

Gero asked, "Were you afraid for your life at that point?"

"Oh, yes," Schiller testified. "Oh, he let me know he would kill me, yes. And I felt like he was going to kill me. I prepared myself to die that night. It wasn't my time, but I was ready. As ready as you can get."

"Did you switch vehicles at some point?" Gero asked.

"Yeah. After the dump, the Orange Field dump, he took me to a house, which I thought was where he lived. He got out and I was still tied up, and he kept threatening to kill me. He then switched vehicles. He got out of his truck and got into a smaller car. He put me in the back seat."

"Did he drive you somewhere else in that car?"

"Yes," Schiller testified. "We left there, and he went to a Jiffy Mart, a little convenience store. I was still tied up in the back and blindfolded."

"Did he threaten you at the Jiffy Mart?"

"Oh, yes," Schiller answered. "That was constant. He was going to kill me. And he did have a gun. He had a gun in his truck, so I had no doubt he would kill me, really."

"After the Jiffy Mart did he drive to another location?"

"Yeah. He brought me over the state line into Louisiana. He knew his secluded places, that's for sure. He brought me into the woods, in the swamps in Louisiana."

"How did you know you were crossing into Louisiana?" Gero asked.

"It's where I grew up, and we were right on the border of Louisiana and Texas. And Louisiana is just right there, not even ten minutes away. And I could tell where we were going. I knew we were going into Louisiana. And that was scary, because there's nothing but swamps in Louisiana."

"At some point did he pull over?"

"Yeah," Schiller answered. "We went into the woods in Louisiana."

"Was it nighttime?" Gero asked.

"Yes, it was nighttime."

"What happened after he stopped the car?"

"I think a car pulled up. He started the car and took me to another place in Louisiana."

"Was it still in the woods?" Gero asked.

"We were in the swamps," Schiller stated. "It was like he knew these places very well and it was secluded and…that was the swamps. Once I went into Louisiana, I definitely didn't feel like I was going home to my mom."

"Did he rape you an additional—"

Schiller interjected, "Oh, yeah. It was—"

"Once?" Gero interrupted. "Or more than once?"

"I don't know how many times," Schiller answered. "It was over and over, until the last time he told me I had to enjoy it, or he was going to kill me."

"Ms. Schiller," Gero said, "is this easy for you to do?"

Sandra Schiller stared hard at Melanson and stated, "No, but I want to do it."

"What was his demeanor?" Gero questioned. "What was his attitude when he was raping you?"

"He was mad," Schiller responded. "He was frustrated and mad and forceful."

"And after he raped you the last time did you talk to him?"

"I talked to him," Schiller replied. "I told him that I'd tell my mom that I ran away, and she would believe me. I told him I had problems at home and, you know, she would believe that I would try to run away and that's where I'd been. And I don't know if he just thought we were going to be friends or what."

"Did he show you his driver's license?"

"Yeah. On the way back from Louisiana where he was going to let me call my dad, he showed me his driver's license. He told me who he was, told me he had been stalking me, and that he was an uncle of a kid I went to school with in the same grade."

Gero then asked, "What was the name on the driver's license he showed you?"

"Roy Melanson."

"At some point did he let you go?"

"Yes, he did," Schiller stated.

"Did he say anything to you before he let you go?"

"Just if I said anything that he'd kill me. And he dropped me off at a telephone and let me call my dad."

"Did you call your dad?"

"Yes, I did," Schiller answered. "I asked him to come and get me."

"Who came to get you?"

"My dad and my brother."

"Were the police notified the next day?"

"Yes."

"Did you give a statement to the police?" Gero inquired.

"Yes."

"Did you end up testifying in court at his trial?"

"Yes, I did," Schiller answered.

"Are you telling the truth today?"

"Yes."

On cross-examination, defense attorney Wilensky probed the witness in an attempt to cast doubt on her credibility. She asked, "Ms. Schiller, each time you were moved you had put your clothes back on in-between?"

"Yes, ma'am," Schiller answered. "He let me put my dress back on."

"And when you got to the next location were you again stripped of your clothes?"

"Yes."

"Did he bind you with your pantyhose?" Wilensky asked.

"Yes. My hands and my legs."

"When you changed from a truck to a car, were your legs still bound?"

"Yes."

"You talked about a time when you honked the horn of the truck to get attention," Wilensky pointed out.

"Yes, in that field, in that first field."

"Were you able to give it several good honks?"

"Oh, yes, ma'am," Schiller said. "I laid on it until he slapped me down."

"Did you struggle or fight back with him at any time?"

"Yes," Schiller testified. "The first time I fought back. It was really the only effort I made to try to get away."

"Do you remember saying Mr. Melanson was balding with salt-and-pepper hair?"

"Yes. He was a gross old man. A dirty old cowboy."

"Did he have strong hands?" Wilensky asked.

"Yes."

Wilensky concluded her cross-examination, realizing that Schiller's recall of the events was unshakeable.

On redirect examination, Gero asked, "You said you remember Mr. Melanson being balding?"

"Receding," Schiller clarified.

"You were seventeen at that time, in 1974?"

"Yes, sir."

"And it's your testimony that Mr. Melanson raped you in February of 1974?"

Schiller responded unequivocally, "Yes, sir."

Retired Policeman Jimmie Smalley

Continuing with his presentation of evidence regarding Melanson's past conduct, Gero next called Jimmie Smalley. Gero asked him to identify himself and tell the jury where he lived and his profession.

"My name is Jimmie Smalley. I live in Pueblo, Colorado, and I worked for the Pueblo Police Department. I retired in 2001."

Gero asked, "Do you remember the Michele Wallace homicide case?"

"I do," Smalley replied. "She was a photographer and a hiker."

"Did you participate in that investigation?"

"I did. On September 12, 1974, an officer stopped a vehicle, and the driver's name was Roy Melanson. A warrants check was made, and it came back for Melanson."

"Did you find anything of significance inside the trunk of his vehicle?"

Smalley testified that they found the registration for the owner, Michele Wallace, of a Mazda vehicle, Mazda car keys, a State Farm insurance card in her father's name, a tool kit for a Mazda and a motor club membership card made out to Michele Wallace.

Smalley went on to testify, "There was a report of a missing person, Michele Wallace, and the person of interest would be Mr. Melanson. We took his wallet and booked it into evidence, along with the other items we found in the trunk. And around September 13, we obtained a pawn ticket dated September 3, 1974, signed by Roy Melanson for a 35-millimeter Canon camera and an extension tube and another lens, and collected these items from the pawn shop."

"Besides this evidence," Gero continued, "did you turn Mr. Melanson himself over to the Gunnison Sheriff's Department?"

"Yes," Smalley testified. "We turned him over on September 13, 1974."

Gero concluded his examination, hoping the jury would take note that was only sixty days after the murder of Anita Andrews.

Retired Sheriff Stephen Fry

It soon became apparent that Jimmie Smalley's testimony had been presented as prelude to the information Gero expected to elicit from his next witness, Stephen Fry. In his introductory testimony, Fry explained that he had been a resident of Gunnison, Colorado, for fifty-nine years. He retired from the Gunnison County Sheriff's Department in 1981 but remembered the Michele Wallace homicide case from when he was the undersheriff.

Gero asked Fry if he recalled when Michele Wallace had been reported missing.

"Her mother reported her missing on September 3, 1974," Fry testified. "Approximately thirty airplanes and some four hundred people were involved in searching the Schofield Park area where Michele was known to have been backpacking, camping and taking photographs as a freelance photographer." Fry then identified Michele Wallace's driver's license photo and confirmed that he had also been looking for her vehicle, a red Mazda with South Carolina license plates, and added, "We were also looking for Roy Melanson because he was the last person seen with Michele."

"Did you end up collecting a hairbrush used by Michele?" Gero asked.

"Yes, I did," Fry replied. "We got it from her apartment, and we stored it in evidence."

Gero continued. "Did the hairbrush become significant?"

"It became significant later, yes."

Gero then asked, "On or about September 18, 1974, did you pick up Mr. Melanson, along with certain evidence from the Pueblo Police Department?"

"Yes, I did."

"Do you recognize Mr. Melanson here in the courtroom?"

Fry pointed to Roy Melanson and described his clothing.

Gero asked several questions to establish that Fry had examined Michele Wallace's vehicle registration and insurance cards, as well as the contents of Roy Melanson's wallet, which included pawn tickets and miscellaneous paper.

"Did all of those papers belong to Mr. Melanson?"

"No, they didn't. They belonged to Michele Wallace," Fry responded.

"Did you ever recover Michele's car?"

"Yeah, her car was found in Amarillo, Texas, by the Amarillo Police Department."

"What about the film removed from the camera given to you by the Pueblo Police Department? Did you ever see the pictures?"

"Yes, I did," Fry stated. "There were photos of Michele and also of her dog. There was also a picture of Roy Melanson with a woman who was later identified as Amy Harvey."

"At some point did the investigation into Michele Wallace's disappearance go cold?"

"It did," Fry answered. "Right after October of 1974 it went cold."

"At that time did you believe Michele was dead?"

"I did."

"What was the first bit of significant evidence uncovered five years later, in 1979?" Gero asked.

"Some people found a scalp up in the Keebler Pass area around Bracken Creek. It had braided hair, and when we sent it for analysis, it was identified as human hair. The hair was later determined to be similar to the hair from Michele's hairbrush."

"Were there additional searches for Michele Wallace's body?"

"Yes. At the time there hadn't been DNA analysis, so the case was reopened in 1990 or 1991."

Gero then asked, "And were Michele Wallace's remains found in 1992?"

"Yes. In 1992 they were found in the Bracken Creek area. And in April, Roy Melanson was arrested for her murder."

"Did you attend Mr. Melanson's murder trial?" Gero pursued.

"Yes, I did. I testified at that trial."

On cross-examination, Wilensky asked, "What was the condition of Michele Wallace's remains when they were recovered in the early 1990s?"

"The body had been buried for years," Fry testified. "At that time, it was just bones, basically."

"Other than bones, scientifically speaking, there was nothing of scientific or forensic value?"

"I believe there were some rotting clothes," Fry stated.

"Was there any way to determine cause of death?"

"Not that I am aware of," Fry said.

"And there was no way to determine the time of death? In essence there was nothing that could be determined about that body except the obvious, that she was deceased. Correct?"

"Yes, that's correct. But on September 1, 1993, in Gunnison, Colorado, Roy Melanson was convicted of the first-degree murder of Michele Wallace."

An awkward pause ensued, and it was apparent Wilensky had not expected the witness to volunteer the fact of Melanson's conviction in response to this particular question. However, it was not really a strategic error on Wilensky's part, as she was doubtless aware of the testimony the jury was scheduled to hear next.

Transcript of Charles Matthews's Testimony Read to Jury

With the permission of the judge, Gero read to the jury Charles Matthews's testimony from the 1993 Michele Wallace homicide trial in Gunnison, Colorado. Matthews had since died, so the reading of his testimony was the only way to bring the information he had provided in the Wallace trial to the jury in the Anita Andrews trial.

In his testimony, Matthews stated that in 1974 he lived in Gunnison, Colorado, after having served in the U.S. Army in Vietnam, where he received three Bronze Stars, a Vietnam campaign medal and an army commendation. In Gunnison, he did ranch work. He recalled in late summer 1974 he met Roy Melanson at the Columbine bar in Gunnison.

Melanson told Matthews he had some horses, and he was having bear trouble in Cumberland Pass. The two of them drove in Matthews's car to the Powderhorn Basin, above Cumberland Pass, to go bear hunting. Matthews retrieved his rifle and saddle at the Powderhorn Basin, and the two men left for the cabin of a friend of Melanson's. Melanson drove most of the time.

It was dark when they got to the cabin, and they both went to bed. The next morning, Matthews said he looked around but didn't see any horses. "The conversation we had the night before didn't really fall into place the next day. Melanson was shying off the horse kick. He didn't seem concerned about it anymore, and we never looked around for horses. We drank a couple of beers, got out the gun, and started shooting up on the side of the hill. On the way back to the cabin that morning, we did begin to look for bear and for horses that Melanson was supposedly renting to someone. He said he was worried about the bear getting his horses, and he was also worried about the guy he was renting horses to."

After hunting for a while, Matthews and Melanson got back in Matthews's car and drove on toward Gunnison. "On the way back, we had car trouble," Matthews testified. "I thought we threw a rod out, so I pulled the car over, locked it up, and we started walking to Gunnison. This car came up behind us.…[I]t was a girl, and she offered us a ride on into town. Her name was Michele. Melanson got in the front seat with her, and I got in the back with the girl's German shepherd."

Matthews then identified a photograph the prosecuting attorney showed him of Michele Wallace and her dog. Matthews testified that Melanson and Michele were talking as they drove, but he didn't remember what they talked about. "When we reached Gunnison, I asked Michele if she could drop me off at the Columbine bar, and she did."

The prosecutor asked, "Did she drop Melanson off, too?

"No. Melanson asked Michele to take him someplace. I didn't really hear the conversation, so I don't know where. I got out of the car at the Columbine bar, and they drove off. Michele was driving, and Melanson was in the front passenger seat. The dog was also in the car."

Matthews further testified that he didn't know Michele's last name at that time, but one morning shortly after he last saw her, he heard on the radio news that a girl was missing. "I wasn't paying too much attention until they mentioned a dog. And then it just struck me."

Sometime that morning, Matthews called Sheriff Porterfield in Gunnison and told him about a girl with a dog who had given him and Melanson a ride to Gunnison. Later, he went to the Sheriff's Department and talked to them. He didn't remember the exact conversations he had with the FBI or with Stephen Fry of the Sheriff's Department, but he did remember telling them what he knew. He was shown a picture of a dog, which he recognized as Michele Wallace's German shepherd.

Matthews was then shown a picture of a man and asked if he recognized the person in that photograph. Matthews said he knew that person as Roy Melanson and that he was the person he met at the Columbine bar in Gunnison. He said that Melanson was the last person he saw with Michele Wallace.

Transcript of Katherine Ortiz's Testimony Read to the Jury

Gero now shifted the jury's attention to a third instance of Melanson's past behavior, which he hoped would help the jury assess the man's character and propensity to commit a crime such as the Anita Andrews murder. The judge had earlier ruled that the rape of Katherine Ortiz was highly substantiating of the charged offense because of striking similarities with the Andrews murder. Both Ortiz and Andrews were isolated and vulnerable, they were both punched in the face and their pants and undergarments were removed from just one leg during the assault.

Gero brought in the information by reading testimony from a prior criminal hearing given by a witness who was now deceased. Katherine Ortiz had testified in Orange County, Texas, on August 21, 1972, regarding an incident that had occurred less than two weeks before, on August 8.

Ortiz had been driving from her brother's house in Bridge City, Texas, to Club 88 in Port Arthur when her tire blew out. Approximately ten minutes later, Roy Melanson and a teenager drove by in a pickup truck and pulled over to offer assistance.

At this point, the prosecutor had asked Ortiz if she could point out the driver of the truck. Ortiz pointed to a person in the audience who was not Roy Melanson. It is unclear whether Ortiz misheard the question and thought she was supposed to identify the truck passenger or if she really did identify someone other than Melanson as the driver of the truck.

She then testified that Melanson drove her to a house to get a spare tire, and somewhere on the way back to her car, he dropped the teenager off. Melanson, now alone with Ortiz, pulled into a clearing off the road and said, "I'm going to fuck you."

"Those were his exact words," she testified. "And I was scared."

She started fighting him, and he fought back, punching her with a closed fist on the left side of her chin, stunning her, and she stopped fighting. "When he repeated what he was going to do to me," she testified, "I told him he'd have to kill me." She began struggling again and said she felt like she was fighting for her life.

Melanson pulled her trousers down completely off one of her legs and down to the knee on the other leg, leaving her underwear on one leg. Ortiz stated she was underneath him when he forced intercourse by penetrating her vagina. Later, after another violent struggle, he penetrated her rectum. "I couldn't fight his strength," she testified.

Melanson forced her to perform fellatio on him, and then he resumed raping her vaginally. After he finished, Ortiz said she tried to pull herself up, but it was difficult. In an attempt to survive, she said she tried to humor him. She had some Kleenex and gave him some, which he used to clean himself. Ortiz cleaned herself as well and dropped her Kleenex out the window, hoping it would be found. She also threw her underwear out the window and then put her slacks back on.

"Melanson was still not dressed," Ortiz testified. "He then started apologizing, and he kept apologizing over and over. We continued to sit there in the dark, and I started to humor him, saying, 'You can be a gentleman, after all.'"

After a while he put his pants on, started the car and drove them "back up and over the bridge, the same one we came in on. He continued to apologize.

When he got back on the paved highway, he drove to Billups, a service station, continuing to apologize." He got the spare tire fixed at the service station and drove them to Rainbow Bridge where Ortiz's car was. There, Melanson changed her tire.

While he was doing this, Ortiz looked at his license plate. "It was my one aim to get his truck back under the light, and then I wanted to see his face and see that license plate and never forget it." She said she also tried to remember the make of his truck.

Melanson told her to follow him back to Bridge City. It was now around 2:00 a.m., when Club 88 closed. She recognized a car belonging to her brother's friend Tiny Richardson, the owner of Club 88. She started her car while Melanson was still talking to her. She did not believe he noticed her brother's friend.

Melanson started to leave, telling Ortiz to follow him, as he wanted to get her safely home. She noticed in her rear-view mirror that Tiny Richardson had stopped his vehicle and made a U-turn to come back. She believed it was to check on her.

Tiny pulled up behind her. Ortiz stopped her car under an underpass, and Tiny caught up to her. Melanson's truck was still ahead of her but going slow. Ortiz rolled down her window, and Tiny asked if she was having trouble. She told him she *was* having trouble, and Tiny said he would follow her home.

By now, Melanson had noticed Ortiz talking to Tiny, and he took off. "I haven't seen him since," she testified. "I haven't seen him since then, until right now."

Tiny followed Katherine to her brother's house, where she told Tiny she had been forcibly raped. She then went into her brother's house and called the police.

EVIDENCE OF PRIOR CONVICTIONS

Gero had now presented all the witnesses he was going to present. Some of Melanson's past crimes could be proved through entering certified copies of the written convictions into evidence. Accordingly, he now presented this documentary evidence of Melanson's September 1, 1993 conviction for Michele Wallace's murder as well as his convictions for the October 13, 1975 aggravated rape of Susan Arnold and the October 11, 1963 rape of Rhonda T.

The judge then gave final instructions on the law to the jury and excused them until the following day, September 29, when closing arguments would be heard.

The anticipation was palpable.

28

CLOSING ARGUMENTS

SEPTEMBER 29, 2011

CLOSING ARGUMENT OF PROSECUTING ATTORNEY PAUL GERO

The judge called on the prosecution to deliver its closing argument. Prosecuting attorney Paul Gero rose, moved to a spot directly in front of the jury box and wasted no time in getting to the facts of the case. Roy Melanson sat quietly at the defense table beside defense attorney Allison Wilensky, betraying no emotion as Gero explained to the jury why he believed the evidence showed beyond reasonable doubt that Melanson was guilty of first-degree murder.

"Wednesday, July 10, 1974, was the last day of Anita Andrews's life," Gero began. "She came home from her secretarial job at Napa State Hospital and then went to Fagiani's Cocktail Lounge, the bar she operated with her sister, Muriel. One of the customers on that date was the defendant, Roy Melanson.

"The place was pretty empty until David Luce, Al Mufich and Al Mackenzie walked in, looking to have a round of beers. They noticed that Anita Andrews was talking to Roy Melanson at the other end of the bar. Melanson turned his back toward the men and hid his face, which Al Mufich took exception to, yelling, 'What the hell are you doing down there?' To make peace, David Luce went up to Melanson, spoke to him and shook his hand.

"Finally, the three men left the bar, leaving Anita Andrews alone with Roy Melanson. She emptied the ashtrays that Luce, Mufich and Mackenzie had used, put away their empty beer bottles, wiped down the counter and pushed in their barstools. Then she walked back to the stockroom. When she walked past Roy Melanson, he punched her in the face and dragged her back into the stockroom. Blood is spurting from her nose, and by now she realizes what is happening and starts to fight for her life.

"Melanson now starts ripping her clothes off. He picks up a bottle and cracks it over her head, and she goes down. Her head is bleeding profusely from a deep laceration, and her skull is fractured. He props her head against a trash can and realizes he might have killed her. He then finds a screwdriver and stabs her thirteen times, all the way from her lungs up to her neck and in one eye.

"He pulls the rings off her fingers, takes her necklace and her wristwatch, steals some money out of the cash box in the office upstairs and walks away. He realizes he's got blood all over him, so he wipes off his hands on a bar towel, throws it on the floor and washes off the screwdriver in the bar sink. Then Roy goes through her purse, grabs her car keys and purse, leaves the bar and hops in her Cadillac."

Looking straight at the jury members, Gero said, "That's why we're here. Your job is to assess the facts and decide what happened that night. In other words, you need to decide what the truth is. And if you decide that a crime has been committed, you are going to apply the law.

"Proof beyond a reasonable doubt is proof that leaves you with an abiding conviction that the murder charge against the defendant is true. You may consider motive or lack of motive. Presence of motive may establish the defendant's guilt; absence of motive may suggest that the defendant is not guilty. We don't have to prove motive, but what could be a motive is Melanson's worry that Anita would report his actions to the police, and he wanted to silence her.

"Now consider David Luce. Thank God for David Luce. With his buddies, David Luce walked into Fagiani's bar that night, and the bar is empty except for one man at the bar, drinking a beer and smoking a cigarette in front of a single ashtray. He's talking to the bartender, Anita Andrews.

"David Luce says this: 'Thirty-seven years later I can still see him sitting there. He's a white adult male, fortyish, a stranger—someone I didn't know. He had a wet hairstyle. He was angled away from us with his back toward us, and he was covering his face like he didn't want us to see him.'

"Luce says that Anita wanted to close the bar, so he and his two friends left, and when they left, only two people were left in the bar: the stranger and Anita Andrews."

Then Gero asked the jury members to turn their attention to criminalist Peter Barnett's testimony. "The murder weapon, the screwdriver, was clean. Drops of blood were found in the bar area near the stockroom, and a smear of blood was found on the inside of the door. In the interior of the stockroom there were blood smears on the trash can and blood spatter on the wall. Anita's pantyhose had been ripped off her body. There were bloody footprints leading up to the cash box in the office, but the cash box was empty.

"As a crime scene reconstructionist, Peter Barnett testified that he believes there was an assault in the bar and that Anita was punched in the face with a closed fist. In the stockroom, glass fragments in Anita's hair showed that she had been hit in the head with a bottle. There was a struggle to the floor, and she was then stabbed with the screwdriver, probably with the right hand because the perpetrator was on top of her and all the stabbing was on her left side.

"Anita died from multiple stab wounds to the chest. I saw thirteen stab wounds, including penetration of her lung and penetration of her left jugular vein. There was a scalp laceration, skull fractures and a subdural hemorrhage, which is bleeding from her brain. Her nose was fractured, and there was a fracture of the hyoid bone, which is in the neck. According to the coroner, it probably took Anita some minutes to die."

Gero then asked the jury the following: "What evidence is there that Roy Melanson committed this murder? Plenty. David Luce identified him. Melanson's DNA was found on the cigarette found in the bar. The bar towel was full of Anita Andrews's blood, and Melanson's DNA was found on that bar towel. The Department of Justice analyzed over a hundred items, including fifty-six DNA samples, and they found two DNA profiles at the crime scene: one was Anita Andrews's DNA. The other was Roy Melanson's. And Melanson was the last person to see Anita Andrews alive."

Gero then reminded the jury of Melanson's criminal history as a rapist and a convicted killer. "You can consider prior crimes to show that he has a disposition to commit such crimes, and you can then conclude that he likely committed the attempted rape and murder of Anita Andrews. She was murdered on July 10, and within sixty days Melanson had murdered Michele Wallace. He isolated Michele in her car, murdered her, then stole her car and her belongings. He was convicted of the first-degree murder of Michele Wallace.

"Five months before that, Melanson raped Sandra Schiller, and two years before *that* he raped Katherine Ortiz. Twelve years before *that* crime, Melanson raped Rhonda T."

Gero then concluded his closing argument with this: "Ladies and gentlemen, I submit to you that Roy Melanson murdered Anita Andrews on July 10, 1974, and I ask that you find him guilty of that murder."

Closing Argument of
Defense Attorney Allison Wilensky

Gero's closing argument lasted less than an hour. After a brief recess, defense attorney Allison Wilensky took Gero's place before the jury to deliver her closing argument. She immediately homed in on what she described as a lack of actual evidence to support Gero's argument. "Mr. Gero painted an interesting picture of what he thinks happened. It's an interesting description of what *might* have happened, but there is no evidence of this. All of Mr. Gero's case is based on guesswork. But a guess is just that, a guess. It's not evidence."

Wilensky then moved to the core of the defense case, informally referred to in defense circles as the "SODDI defense," or "Some Other Dude Did It." That defense rests on the argument that the evidence is insufficient to prove beyond a reasonable doubt that the defendant committed the crime. The SODDI defense is employed in cases where the defense cannot deny that a crime has occurred, such as a homicide. In such a situation, the defense attempts to shift blame onto another unidentified person.

"In this case," Wilensky pointed out, "the premise is that some unknown person came into the bar after Roy Melanson left and killed Anita Andrews. There is no proof beyond a reasonable doubt that my client committed this crime. Yes, Mr. Melanson was at the bar that night. Yes, he is a rapist. He has killed in the same manner, and he is a liar.

"So he was in the bar that night. But look where his fingerprints were found—on empty bottles that had been put back in a box to go to the stockroom. And there's the DNA evidence, in this case the DNA evidence on a cigarette butt and a bloody bar towel. However, when forensic serologist Gary Harmor tested this DNA, he found only a partial match. A *partial* match. So, Mr. Gero would have you use Gary Harmor's testimony about the DNA evidence on this bloody towel as proof that Mr. Melanson's DNA was found behind the bar.

"We know from senior criminalist Michelle Terra that simply breathing over the evidence causes contamination. Do we know what happened with that bar towel? Here's the problem with that bloody towel: What the experts did with this bloody towel is they cut pieces out of it from all over the towel, and Mr. Harmor told you that he made an assumption that only one person had touched that towel. Where is the evidence to support this assumption? We can't guess what happened with that towel the whole rest of the day. We don't know how many people touched that towel. We know that towel had other male DNA, and it wasn't Mr. Melanson's.

"So, what are we left with? Mr. Melanson was in the bar. That's all we know. We know that the lab we are dealing with had enormous levels of contamination before and during the time this towel was tested. In testing this item itself there was contamination. And yet the prosecutor wants you to trust this evidence."

Wilensky then turned the jury's attention to the reliability of the testimony of witness David Luce. "David Luce is a man who, by his own admission, hangs out in bars, gets in plenty of fights, and hangs out with loud and abusive men. He is a man who can't remember the people or the police officers he talked to over the years. He's a man who can't remember telling people that he'd never be able to identify the person he saw in the bar. He's a man who doesn't remember how many bars he went to that night. This is the man who the next day doesn't remember what bar he's in, let alone how much he had to drink. Why is this important? We know Mr. Melanson was at the bar. Thirty-seven years later, all of a sudden David Luce remembers oh, yeah, Mr. Melanson was hiding his face. Suddenly David Luce's memory has gotten better. Really? Does it even make sense?

"We know that Mr. Melanson was in the bar for a fairly long time. Other people saw him in the bar. Other people gave descriptions; that's what the police officers told us. Somebody saw Mr. Melanson pour a drink. Is that the man who's all of a sudden hiding his face? That doesn't make sense. If a man doesn't want to be seen, he doesn't sit in a bar full of patrons for hours and hours helping himself to alcohol. It doesn't make sense. It doesn't make sense because it didn't happen. Even if thirty-seven years later, Mr. Luce suddenly remembers that it did happen."

Wilensky next took on the difficult task of framing, for the jury, Melanson's criminal history. "Mr. Melanson is a rapist. He is. You have the 1962 conviction. You have a 1975 conviction. And you've got a case without a conviction. The testimony of Katherine Ortiz that was read to you was lengthy, but one thing stood out for me: When Katherine Ortiz was asked to identify the man in the courtroom who had raped her, she pointed to somebody in the audience.

"Yes, Mr. Melanson is a convicted rapist. But the prosecutor is asking you to guess that he raped Katherine Ortiz, too. Mr. Gero wants you to keep guessing at all these things because sooner or later it's gonna pile up and you're gonna be overwhelmed with evidence. But you know what? You can't guess. Mr. Gero would have to prove, by a preponderance of the evidence, that the rape of Katherine Ortiz was committed by Mr. Melanson. Mr. Gero hasn't proved that because Ms. Ortiz did not identify Mr. Melanson at the trial.

"Mr. Gero told you that Roy Melanson killed Anita Andrews because he'd committed all those other rapes and he was tired of getting caught. He didn't want to be identified. Really? The first rape was in 1962. He was convicted of that rape. Sandra Schiller's rape occurred before 1974, and he didn't kill Sandra Schiller. You know what? Ms. Schiller's conviction wasn't until after 1974. What Mr. Gero said makes no sense.

"But here's the big one. My client is a convicted murderer. That's true. You have two kinds of cases, two pieces of evidence about who Mr. Melanson is. The first one is the evidence of rape. And it's true you can absolutely use that. I think somebody said that a tiger doesn't change its stripes. The theory is that once a rapist, always a rapist. However, that by itself is not sufficient to prove that Mr. Melanson is guilty of the murder of Anita Andrews. The prosecution must still prove that the person in this case is guilty beyond a reasonable doubt. Mr. Gero hopes that your emotions come into play, that you decide that, while there might be sufficient evidence, Mr. Melanson is the murderer because he is a rapist. You can't do that. The law doesn't let you. You must follow the law and decide based on the evidence.

"In evaluating the Michele Wallace murder, the law tells us to consider the similarity or lack of similarity between that case and the Anita Andrews case. The jury can look for a common plan or scheme. It's kind of like a signature or a calling card. Are two crimes so similar that you say, wow, there's something going on here? There's a pattern?

"But there is no common plan or scheme for these two murders. Circumstances in each case show the lack of similarity. In the Wallace murder we don't know the cause of death. We don't know how she died. Was she strangled? Stabbed? Beaten? You don't know because there's no evidence. And you cannot speculate. You cannot guess, so there's a lack of similarity. In that case there is absolutely no evidence of rape. None. All we know is that Michele Wallace was dead. Also, that murder occurred out on a road in an isolated area, not in a bar where other people were around. There's no similarity there. None at all.

"In addition, Michele Wallace was a young woman of seventeen [*sic*, Michele Wallace was twenty-five years old]. Anita Andrews was fifty-one. No similarities there. In the Michele Wallace case, the deceased's body was put someplace where it took many years to find. It was hidden, dumped someplace where it would not be found. Anita Andrews was left on the floor of her bar, where she was almost certain to be discovered within a very short time.

"You cannot consider the fact that Mr. Melanson has murdered before and assume that therefore he did it again. You must follow the law, and the law says that unless you find those crimes so similar that it's obvious they had to have been committed by the same person, you can't consider that homicide at all. In this case, a car is missing, and a woman is dead. That's all there is. Age, location, time, everything is different. So, you cannot consider that they are related. There is no common plan or scheme.

"The prosecutor also asked you to consider other similarities. He told you in his story that Mr. Melanson ripped off Anita's rings, took her watch and a necklace. He stated there was a missing purse, missing cash. But he produced no evidence that those things happened. Whereas in the Michele Wallace case we know Mr. Melanson took things because we have the pawn tickets. We have no such evidence in this case, and a guess by any other name is still a guess. Detective Jarecki documented the bar items that were taken and turned over to Anita's sister, Muriel. What was listed? A black purse and $206 in cash, so clearly there *was* money in the bar. Finally, even with evidence of a prior rape or homicide, the prosecutor must still prove his case beyond a reasonable doubt."

Wilensky then turned her attention to Melanson's interview with Detective Winegar. "Melanson said he had never been in Napa. But Mr. Melanson was a drifter, and thirty-seven years later he probably doesn't remember every town he had ever been in or traveled through. And, apart from having an awful lot of bars, Napa in 1974 wasn't a tourist attraction. There was nothing memorable about Napa in 1974. It was just another spot on the road. When Mr. Melanson said, 'I swear on my mother's grave I got nothing to do with what you're talking about,' remember that at that point Detective Winegar is not just saying we have your fingerprints. He's saying we have your blood, your DNA, which basically shows that you committed this crime. And Mr. Melanson says no. The fact that Mr. Melanson lied, saying he hadn't been in Napa, is not proof that he committed this murder. The prosecutor hasn't provided you with proof."

Recalling the legal standard of "beyond a reasonable doubt," Wilensky concluded her argument by raising doubts. "There's one big question here. One big question. What happened when David Luce and his friends left the bar? The prosecutor told you that Anita was intending to close the bar. Well, that's what David Luce thought. But where is the evidence? And what if she *did* intend to close the bar? Who's to say that someone Anita knew didn't stop by the bar that night after Mr. Melanson left? What if somebody Anita didn't know came in because they didn't know the bar was closed? Who's to say that somebody who had already been at the bar didn't come back? We don't know. *You* don't know. The prosecutor assumes Mr. Melanson was the only man in town that night, not just the only man in the bar. If the doors weren't locked, you don't know what happened.

"What if the killer *didn't* leave his DNA at the bar? What if the only DNA found at the bar is from people who drank there that night? You don't know what happened, and you can't guess. The prosecutor says the bar was spotless and nobody else came in after David Luce and his friends left.

"There's a photograph the prosecutor presented that I found particularly interesting. It's a photograph of the stairs, where there was a drop of blood. You know what? The photograph also showed a bottle, and around that bottle is a napkin, as if somebody held that bottle and drank from it with the napkin between their fingers and the glass. But I have a question. Where is that bottle? Mr. Gero says the bar was exactly as it was left. Really? I'd like to know about that bottle. Because if Anita was cleaning up and she was on her way out, why is there a bottle wrapped in a napkin on the stairs? What if another person had come into the bar?

"If you recall, not long before this happened Anita called her friend Joe Silva and asked him to come to the bar and pretend he was her boyfriend because she said there was a creep in the bar. It happened just that once? Ironically, if you recall, Anita Andrews indicated that Mr. Melanson was her boyfriend when David Luce asked. Maybe she thought David Luce and his friends were creeps. There's no way to know.

"And that's where this case is. You don't know. Yes, Mr. Melanson was there. But beyond that, you have only guesses, no actual evidence. And once you set your emotions aside, there is only one verdict you can reach in this case, and that is not guilty."

Rebuttal Argument of Prosecutor Paul Gero

In a criminal case, the prosecution bears the burden of proving the defendant's guilt beyond a reasonable doubt. Because of this burden, the law provides the prosecuting attorney two opportunities to argue before the jury: an initial closing argument and a rebuttal argument after the defense attorney's closing argument.

Prosecuting attorney Paul Gero rose to present his rebuttal to Wilensky's closing argument. "Circumstantial evidence does not directly prove a fact to be decided; rather, it is evidence of another fact or group of facts from which you may logically and reasonably conclude the truth of the matter in question. So what the defense attorney is saying is that this case is based on circumstantial evidence, therefore you can't make any logical or reasonable inferences, also known as guesswork. So you're supposed to throw up your hands and say well, there wasn't a confession or a videotape, and Mr. Melanson's semen wasn't found on the victim, therefore it's all circumstantial evidence and everything else in the case is just a bunch of guesses.

"The SODDI defense, also known as Some Other Dude Did It, is common. Of course, it is possible that some other dude *did* do it, but it's not reasonable. The evidence points to Mr. Melanson.

"Ms. Wilensky argues that there's no semen anywhere, there's no eyewitness, there's no direct evidence, therefore we should throw up our hands and say there's not enough evidence here so it's all guesswork. Ms. Wilensky says David Luce is a liar. If you thought that David Luce completely fabricated his testimony for some unknown reason, you should acquit Mr. Melanson. But David Luce has nothing to gain here. He's just telling you what he believes. He's trying to do the right thing.

"This trial is a search for the truth, for a verdict based on the evidence, not on speculation. It's now your job to determine what happened. We gave you everything to consider. There's been great detective work here. There's been great forensic science used in this case. So if there's something you're not comfortable with, disregard that piece of evidence and look at the rest of the evidence. You tell me, just based on logical inference, is this case based on guesswork? Or is it based on what's reasonable?

"This is what's reasonable. Melanson is a rapist. Anita is alone, and he sees an opportunity. He waits for David Luce and his two friends to leave. Anita wants to close the bar, but Melanson punches her in the face and pulls her into the stockroom. There's a violent struggle in which he attempts to rape her and ends up stabbing her with a screwdriver. He cleans up, he robs her, he takes her car and he ends up in Colorado. That's completely reasonable.

"Now let's talk about what's *unreasonable*, the Some Other Dude Did It defense and the random creep theory. Mr. Melanson, a rapist who raped a woman a few months before the Anita Andrews murder, is hanging out at Fagiani's bar. He is hiding his face from the other bar patrons for no reason, he just happens to be doing that on that day. Mr. Melanson is alone with Anita, but it's time to go, so he's gonna leave. She cleans up the entire bar except for his ashtray and his cigarette butt and restoring his barstool. He gets up and walks out, and she's there by herself in the empty bar. The real killer, also a rapist, comes in right after Mr. Melanson. What a coincidence! And that real killer, who was never seen by anyone, attempts to rape Anita, kills her and steals her car. The real killer leaves no DNA or fingerprints at the crime scene, leaves Napa and disappears forever.

"Mr. Melanson also leaves Napa, and he leaves the state. And then by coincidence, less than two months later, he also happens to kill another woman and steal her car. And then thirty-seven years later, when he's confronted by the police, he doesn't say, 'Yeah, I went to Napa, maybe I remember being in some bar in Napa, but I didn't kill anyone, I don't know what you're talking about.' Instead, he says, 'I've never been to Napa in my life.'

"Is that reasonable? No, that is completely unreasonable. Melanson is lying. So, let's look at some other things that are unreasonable. Melanson leaves the bar, so why doesn't Anita push his barstool in? Why doesn't she empty his ashtray? Why does he not realize that someone was murdered at the bar that night, as David Luce did, and tell someone that he was also in that bar on that night?

"Why would Anita let anyone else inside the bar? She clearly wanted to go home. She gets rid of the three guys; she gets rid of Mr. Melanson. Why doesn't she go home at that point? Why does she have her shoes on as if she's ready to go home? Now if Melanson is enjoying a nice stay in Napa, or coming through town, does he go back home? No. He doesn't live in Napa. Does he go back to a hotel? There's no evidence he was staying in a hotel. Why all of a sudden does he leave town after Anita is murdered?

"So, is it unreasonable to assume that the real killer is outside looking through Fagiani's window, sees Melanson leave and thinks here's my opportunity? He leaves no DNA at the crime scene, no fingerprints. He's lucky, because Mr. Melanson left *his* DNA on the bar towel. Or does the real killer happen to have the same DNA profile as Mr. Melanson?

"Is that reasonable? Sure, it's *possible*, but is it *reasonable*? I don't think so. It is not reasonable that there's another man like Mr. Melanson who likes to rape women, likes to murder women and likes to steal cars, and he just happened to come into the same bar after Mr. Melanson leaves. That is completely unreasonable. It is *possible*, yes. But it is not *reasonable*.

"We are here because Anita Andrews was murdered, and Roy Melanson committed this murder in the first degree. I ask you to convict him of that crime."

29

JURY DELIBERATIONS AND THE VERDICT

With the closing arguments complete, the time had come for the judge to turn the case over to the jury. He began by providing them with guidance on the laws they were to apply, including the specific things that would have to have been proved for the defendant to be convicted of murder in the first or second degree. He then told the jury that the bailiff would usher them to the jury room and that their first order of business would be to select a foreperson. Then they would need to begin their deliberations.

The jury members commenced their review of the evidence in the early afternoon of Thursday, September 29, 2011.

Most of the courtroom staff—clerks, bailiffs and the court reporter—expected a quick verdict and a speedy conviction. Some spectators were so confident of a short deliberation they didn't leave the courthouse. The attorneys returned to their offices, and the prosecutor's investigator and deputies disassembled the PowerPoint equipment used to present visual evidence and removed it. Roy Melanson was taken back to the jail. He would be brought back into the courtroom only when the jurors finished their deliberations.

Although the case against Melanson appeared to be strong, some court observers felt that defense attorney Wilensky had done a credible job in raising reasonable doubt for the jurors to consider, arguing effectively that while the defendant had a significant criminal record, the evidence against him was thin, circumstantial and therefore weak. Even if Wilensky failed to convince all twelve jurors, it would take only one juror voting for acquittal to result in a hung jury. In that event, the entire case would have to be retried or dropped altogether.

By 4:30 p.m. that afternoon there was no verdict. Instead, the jury informed the judge they were going to take a break for the balance of the evening and continue their deliberations at 8:45 a.m. the following morning.

On Friday, September 30, 2011, the jury members reassembled and continued their deliberations. The morning progressed, and still there was no verdict. Now there was buzz around the courthouse that perhaps one or more jury members might have reasonable doubt.

Noon arrived, still without a verdict. At 4:30 p.m., the jury met with the judge to discuss how to proceed if it did not reach a verdict before the end of the day. The jury foreman felt they were close to reaching a verdict, and he requested that the judge allow them to continue deliberations because the foreman indicated they might use the next half hour productively. The judge granted the request but admonished them not to rush their verdict.

At 4:55 p.m. that Friday evening, after seven-plus hours of deliberation, the jury asked the bailiff to let the judge know a verdict had been reached. The judge had the court clerk call the trial attorneys, who returned to the courtroom within minutes. Melanson was brought from the jail holding cell by the correctional officers, who transferred him to the bailiffs in the courtroom. They had him resume his seat next to his attorney at the attorneys' table. The clerks, bailiffs and judge then filed into the courtroom.

In the courtroom were staff attorneys from both the district attorney and public defender offices, the press and some interested spectators. Also present were some law enforcement officers, in particular Detective Winegar and Investigator Severe, who had hurried to the courtroom to hear the verdict. The judge directed the bailiff to bring the jury into the courtroom. Up until this moment, there were whispered conversations among those present. The murmurs ceased once the jury was seated in the jury box.

The judge asked the foreman to hand the verdict to the bailiff, who promptly brought it to the judge. The judge read the verdict silently, checking to ensure that it was completed, dated and signed by the foreman. The judge handed the verdict to his clerk and asked her to read the verdict aloud. By now the courtroom was completely silent.

The jury found Roy Melanson guilty of murder in the first degree. That verdict brought closure to a thirty-seven-year-old murder case that few people thought would ever be solved.

Roy Melanson betrayed no emotion as he heard the verdict. The judge separately addressed each member of the jury, asking if the guilty verdict was indeed his or her individual judgment. All twelve jurors answered in the affirmative. The judge thanked the jury members for their service and dismissed them. Their work complete, the jurors stood and filed quietly out of the courtroom.

As Detective Winegar left the courtroom after the verdict was read, he encountered *Napa Valley Register* reporter Kerana Todorov. She later wrote, "Winegar recalled telling the victim's sister, Muriel Fagiani, in November 2009, a year before her death, that a person had been identified in the matter of Anita's murder. Muriel was pleased, Winegar said.

"But Muriel also said that it wouldn't bring her sister back.

"'And that's the truth,' Winegar added."

30

SENTENCING

THURSDAY, OCTOBER 27, 2011

The Probation Department report recommended that Roy Melanson be sentenced to the period prescribed by law. After reviewing the aggravating and mitigating circumstances of the case, the defendant's background and the impact of the crime on the victim or victims, probation officers may recommend a sentence within the minimum and maximum penalties provided for the crime committed. The maximum sentence, using 1974 sentencing laws, was twenty-five years to life imprisonment. The death penalty was not an option.

Often in a high-profile case, the courtroom is packed with spectators on the day of the defendant's sentencing. On this day, however, the courtroom had few spectators. Present were the courtroom clerks, the court reporter and two court bailiffs. *Napa Valley Register* reporter Kerana Todorov was present, as were a few deputy public defenders in support of defense attorney Allison Wilensky and several deputy district attorneys in support of Paul Gero. Detective Don Winegar and Investigator Leslie Severe were also present. Both had been an integral part of prosecuting attorney Paul Gero's team.

But there was no crowd of relatives or friends seeking justice for Anita Andrews and insisting that the judge deliver the stiffest possible sentence to Roy Melanson. Muriel Fagiani, the sister of the victim, had passed away the year before the trial. Anita Andrews's two daughters made it clear that they each cared deeply about justice being meted out to Roy Melanson, but rather than appear in the courtroom on this day, they wrote letters to the judge. These were attached to the Probation Department report. Neither daughter could bear to revive the painful memories of their mother's murder, nor did they wish to ever see their mother's killer again.

Roy Melanson, dressed in a blue jail jumpsuit and shackled in a wheelchair, was wheeled one last time to the counsel table next to his defense attorney, Allison Wilensky. Prosecuting attorney Paul Gero took his seat opposite the defense attorney at the counsel table, alongside his investigators, Detective Don Winegar and Leslie Severe.

The judge opened the proceeding by announcing that he had received, read and considered the Napa probation officer's written report. He then asked the attorneys if they had also received and read the report and whether they were prepared to proceed with formal sentencing. Both attorneys indicated they were ready to proceed.

Paul Gero then read aloud the letters from Anita Andrews's two daughters, both of whom had been young adults when their mother was killed. In these letters, both daughters wrote of the pain they and their families had endured over the past thirty-seven years.

The attorneys then indicated to the judge that neither had anything further to say. Folding his hands on the desk, the judge leaned in the defendant's direction and sentenced Roy Melanson to life in prison. He was careful to note that the sentence was being imposed in accordance with the laws in effect in 1974, when the crime had been committed, and he went on to rule that this sentence would be served consecutively, not concurrently, to the life term imposed in the state of Colorado. This meant that Melanson wouldn't start serving the new sentence until he had completed the life sentence in Colorado for the 1974 murder of hiker and freelance photographer Michele Wallace.

The judge then explained the rules regarding the appeal of criminal convictions in California and asked Melanson if he understood that he had the right to appeal his case within sixty days.

Melanson answered, "Yes, sir."

There was a brief pause while Melanson engaged in a whispered conversation with Allison Wilensky. When this was concluded, and it

Roy Melanson. *Courtesy of the Napa County District Attorney's Office.*

became apparent that Wilensky did not intend to further address the court, the judge ordered that Melanson be returned to the custody of the Napa sheriff to await transportation back to prison in Colorado. The court bailiffs wheeled him out of the courtroom and back to the jail.

In a *Napa Valley Register* news article appearing later that day, reporter Kerana Todorov wrote, "[A]fter the sentencing, defense attorney Allison Wilensky stated that her client will file an appeal. 'It is his right,' she said. 'That's what he wants.'"

In the same newspaper article, prosecuting attorney Paul Gero was quoted as stating, "Melanson is up for parole on the Colorado murder sentence in September 2012. Today's sentence ensures that he's not getting out of prison. If Colorado releases Roy Melanson from prison, he must return to California to serve today's life sentence."

The consecutive life sentence had ensured that the seventy-four-year-old killer would die in prison.

Only a serial rapist knows how many rapes he has committed, and only a serial killer knows how many victims have died at his hands. It is possible that Roy Melanson may enlighten us about such events while there is still life in him, but it is much more probable that his secrets will die with him.

31

WHEN A MURDER IS COMMITTED

When a murder is committed, the consequences are far-reaching and are not limited to the actual victim. As any law enforcement officer will attest, when people learn that a loved one has been killed, they are changed forever. The grief can be so profound the victim's relatives or friends are unable to heal. The world as they know it has collapsed. The survivors emerge dazed, and the person they were before the murder is gone forever.

Such was the case for the family of Anita Andrews

Anita Andrews was fifty-one years old when she was murdered, young enough that she and her family still had much to look forward to. Her two daughters, then in their twenties, had expected to have their mother's love and support as they moved through their young adult years and started families of their own. Anita had been her sister Muriel's closest living relative, and the two enjoyed a unique relationship, which Muriel had assumed would continue into their old age.

In a letter to the judge at the time of sentencing, one of Anita's daughters wrote that finding the murderer and securing his conviction was not a time for joy or relief. The pain merely continued, as it forced her to confront her mother's brutal death yet again. She grieved for the thirty-seven years that had passed without being able to share her joys and sorrows with her mother. She remembered being raised by a single parent and described her mother as being the glue that kept the family members close to one another, close to relatives and close to their father's family.

This daughter also lamented the suffering of her own two children, Anita's grandchildren. Anita never had the joy of watching them grow up, and they would never know their grandmother.

Since the violent death of her mother, this daughter had suffered physically. She developed an irregular racing heartbeat of over two hundred beats per minute that required medication.

In another letter to the judge, Anita's other daughter wrote about being filled with fear that someone might commit another such violent act. She grew afraid to trust anyone because she could never be sure whether a person who was initially nice to you might not then kill you. Her anxiety and her fears were endless.

This daughter also mourned the specific losses that accompanied her mother's murder: no more mother-daughter chats or phone calls or family reunions. No more "cute little cards for silly occasions." She wrote that her mother was a good woman, a wonderful mom, a nice person, a hard worker and that she never said a bad thing about anyone. Her mother always tried to do the best she could for everyone.

Anita's death greatly affected her sister, Muriel Fagiani. Muriel was devastated by her sister's murder, and she never fully recovered. She spent the rest of her days urging the authorities to solve the murder, and she never gave up. Until the end of her life, she hoped that her only sister's murderer would be caught, and it is unfortunate that she passed away without knowing that the killer would be tried and convicted.

In the case of Roy Melanson, there had been numerous victims, accompanied by the inevitable agony of families, loved ones and friends.

Such is the legacy of a serial killer.

After Melanson was identified as a suspect in the murder of Anita Andrews, Investigator Leslie Severe conducted a background profile on him before and after his July 1974 appearance in Napa. She located and spoke to an elderly woman by the name of Rhonda T., and when Severe told her why she was calling, Rhonda began to cry. She confided that she had never shared with her family what had happened to her. Even her husband did not know that Roy Melanson had raped her.

In 1962, Rhonda T. had been working for a family in Texas. One night after leaving work, Melanson pulled her over as if he were the police, pulled her out of her car and raped her. She was shattered. She told Severe that the family she worked for tried to help her, and on March 29, 1962, Roy Melanson was convicted of the rape. Rhonda T. later married and had a family, but she kept that secret for her entire life. The facts of this rape, and the devastation to Rhonda T. and her family, were not brought out in the trial because prosecutor Gero needed to prove only that Melanson had been convicted of her rape. He did this by presenting documentary evidence of Melanson's conviction, which spared Rhonda T. from having to appear in court.

In the case of Michele Wallace, the twenty-five-year-old woman who came to Gunnison, Colorado, in the summer of 1974 to photograph the Rocky Mountains, the consequences of her murder were truly tragic.

Michele went missing on August 30, 1974, approximately six weeks after Anita Andrews was murdered. Two weeks later, Michele's grieving mother committed suicide. She left a note saying she wanted to go to heaven and be with Michele, and that if her daughter was ever found, she asked her husband, George Wallace, to bury Michele's body next to hers.

Melanson murdered Michele, but he was not arrested and convicted until many years later. Tragically, had he been tracked down and caught in the days following Anita Andrews's murder, he would not have been free to kill Michele Wallace.

In August 1992, eighteen years after Michele Wallace's disappearance, a forensic odontologist confirmed that her dental records matched teeth in the skull found during a search conducted by law enforcement agents and scientists who volunteered to help police agencies find human remains. Alisha Wyman's article in the March 22, 2010 *Napa Valley Register* titled "Two Women Who May Share a Common Killer" stated that after Melanson's trial and conviction, Michele's father, George Wallace, buried his daughter's remains in the same grave as his wife's, as she had wished. On Michele's birthday in the mid-1990s, he held a funeral for her.

Gunnison County Sheriff's Department investigator Kathy Ireland was credited with solving the Wallace murder case. She attended the funeral service and said that, even though a couple of decades had passed since Michele's death, she was amazed at the number of high school classmates and other friends who were there.

In February 1974, five months before Anita Andrews was murdered, Melanson raped Sandra Arnold. Haskell Taylor, now a retired Texas Ranger, said that Melanson had come across a woman with a flat tire on a road in Texas. He fixed the tire, then beat the woman and raped her.

In a March 2010 *Napa Valley Register* article by staff writer Alisha Wyman titled "A Violent Journey," Haskell Taylor was quoted as saying that Sandra had survived the rape, but she had a nervous breakdown and was later institutionalized.

In the case of twenty-four-year-old Charlotte Sauerwin, the personal consequences went far beyond the murder victim. That crime ruined the lives of two persons: the victim herself and her fiancé at the time of her death, John Lejeune.

On August 5, 1988, Sauerwin was engaged to be married and living in Livingston Parish, Louisiana. She was seen talking to a man who claimed to be "Cajun," smoked cigarettes and was a stranger in the area. Later, she went to a mechanic's shop to pay a bill. She was never seen alive again.

Her fiancé returned home from work that night and made dinner, but Sauerwin did not come home. At 9:00 p.m., Lejeune called her parents. By 11:00 p.m. Lejeune, along with Sauerwin's parents, had called the police. Three hours later, sheriffs found her body; she had been beaten and strangled, and her neck had been slashed.

Charlene Morris, the sister of Charlotte Sauerwin, said her sister's death caused her family great suffering. According to a June 7, 2010 *Denver Post* article by Joey Bunch titled "Convicted Colorado Killer May Never Be Tried in Other States Despite DNA," Charlene said, "He [Melanson] drove the nails into momma and daddy's coffin. They just shut down after that."

In a June 2, 2010 article, "Fagiani's Murder Suspect Implicated in Louisiana Killing" by *Napa Valley Register* staff writer Alisha Wyman, Charlene Morris explained that after Charlotte Sauerwin's murder her parents never celebrated birthdays or holidays. Family members went their separate ways.

The murder and subsequent investigation were particularly hard on Sauerwin's fiancé, John Lejeune, who was called in for questioning several times after her death. Morris was quoted as saying, "He [Melanson] didn't just take her away from him [Lejeune]. He messed up two families, and we can't repair none of that."

According to reporter Alisha Wyman, for years after Sauerwin's murder, John Lejeune was looked upon in his hometown as the prime suspect. The strain between Sauerwin's and Lejeune's families tore them apart.

The tragic consequences of any murder affect a multitude of people forever. When it involves a serial killer, the consequences become immeasurable. These individuals are only a few of Melanson's victims and their families. There were others, some we know of, and perhaps others that are not yet known.

WHERE ARE THEY NOW?

Where are the participants in this trial today?

The defense attorney, Allison Wilensky, continues to work for the Napa County Public Defender's Office. As a defense attorney, it is her job to fight for the underdog. However, she also fights for the underdog because it is her nature. It is what drives her. She is a hardworking, accomplished and experienced attorney, but she is not a magician. She can only do so much with the hand she is dealt. She doesn't create the facts; she is stuck with them.

In the trial of Roy Melanson for the murder of Anita Andrews, Wilensky worked to punch holes in the prosecution's case in a creditable effort to raise a reasonable doubt in the minds of jury members. She performed this job so well that the jury was in deliberation for almost two days. The jury members ultimately returned a guilty verdict, but it was not because of any inadequacy on the part of the defense attorney.

Many people contributed to the successful prosecution of Roy Melanson. The original Napa Police Department officers, judged in retrospect, did a superb job of obtaining the crime scene evidence and preserving it for decades, retaining some items that at the time they could not have known would be instrumental in convicting the defendant. In 1974, the stub of a cigarette would not be considered likely to produce any usable evidence, but it was retained. That cigarette stub produced the single most important piece of forensic evidence that led to the identification and apprehension of Roy Melanson—his DNA.

The dedication of the Napa Police Department ran deep. The murder of Anita Andrews was never forgotten, and their shared sense of obligation to apprehend her killer was passed on from one generation of police officers to the next. The passage of time did not diminish their pursuit of justice. By the time Roy Melanson went on trial in September 2011, many of the original investigating officers had died, but their work continued to assist in his conviction for first-degree murder.

The trial team for the prosecution was nothing short of excellent. Attorney Paul Gero, Detective Don Winegar and Investigator Leslie Severe worked seamlessly together, each doing his or her part to build a solid case of circumstantial evidence against the defendant. Winegar was primarily in charge of the Napa Police Department work, Gero addressed the research on prior rape and murder cases (both arrests and convictions) and Severe tracked down the individuals involved in those prior cases. Both Winegar and Gero traveled to the prison in Colorado to interview Melanson and subsequently to research the Michele Wallace murder. All three team members traveled to Texas and Louisiana to interview prior rape victims and witnesses and to research other relevant rapes and murders.

Paul Gero had always wanted to be a prosecutor. After law school, he completed internships in the district attorneys' offices in San Francisco, Los Angeles, Marin County and San Mateo. He went on to serve as a deputy district attorney in Lake County, California, from 1998 to 2000, after which he worked in Napa as a deputy district attorney until 2011, before being named chief deputy district attorney. In 2012, Gero was named prosecutor of the Year for the State of California by the California District Attorneys Association. In 2014, he became assistant district attorney in Napa. He remains in that position. Gero is an unusually gifted trial attorney. He is intelligent, he thinks well on his feet and he is always well prepared.

In May 2006, Don Winegar was assigned the Anita Andrews murder investigation. He managed to devote significant time to the cold case while also working a full caseload. Winegar read every past police report, ensured completion of all forensic testing and assembled all the evidence before sending it over to prosecutor Gero.

Winegar had been a Napa Police Department officer since 1987. He is an easygoing, friendly person who rarely loses patience, doesn't let much of anything bother him and is affable and likable. Winegar is everything a professional detective should be, a smart (in both natural intelligence and street smarts), hardworking detective who fights for the oppressed and the mistreated. Over the years, he received several commendations as police officer of the month, as well as commendations for criminal investigations and several public letters of commendation from crime victims.

At the time of the Roy Melanson trial, Winegar was in his early fifties. He is now retired and living with his wife in Palm Beach, Florida, where he enjoys working out at a gym several times a week, playing golf and riding a golf cart around the country club. He also loves to fish for steelhead and salmon. He has five adult children and four grandchildren. His youngest son, Christian, recently graduated from the Napa Valley College Police Academy. When Christian was sworn in as a deputy sheriff at the Napa County Sheriff's Office on June 15, 2019, Don was present and had the honor of pinning on his son's badge.

Though long retired, Winegar still catches himself thinking about a gap in the information about Roy Melanson he had not been able to track down. "My background information on him is missing four months, from April 1974 in Arizona, when he drives away from his pregnant girlfriend, until the July 1974 murder in Napa. I used all my capabilities to find more information during those four months without success, and it still bugs me. During this missing period of time, who did Melanson rape or murder and where? How did he come to be in Napa, at Fagiani's bar? He stole Anita Andrews's Cadillac, bought gas in Sacramento and then what? What happened to her car, and how did Melanson get to Colorado? I don't know these answers, but I would sure like to find out."

Leslie Severe was the main point of contact with witness David Luce. Sometimes a witness will gravitate toward one person on a trial team, and for the elderly and dying Luce, the youthful and engaging Severe was that person. Paul Gero was pleased to have such a competent investigator as Severe, and he had been sure from the outset that Severe and Winegar would work well together. Severe continues to work as an investigator for the Napa County District Attorney's Office, and she is acknowledged as one of the best investigators in the state. In 2014, she was recognized as investigator of the year by the California Investigators Association. She is outgoing and flexible; she is not, however, without opinions, and she gives them when she thinks it necessary. Severe has since married and is now Leslie Pate. With her husband, she loves to go ocean fishing for salmon, lingcod and halibut, and she also enjoys diving, kayaking, running, hiking or doing anything outdoors. Detective Winegar described Leslie this way: "If it was cool and fun she would try it."

Detective Don Winegar pinning the badge on his son Christian as he's sworn in at the Napa County Sheriff's Department ceremony. *Courtesy of Don Winegar.*

Pate is the epitome of what a professional investigator should be; she is smart and focused on her mission and can talk to anyone.

From 1974 to the time of the 2011 trial, the Napa Police Department and the office of the district attorney fought for Anita Andrews. They gave her a voice, and they never gave up. They brought justice for Anita; for her two daughters; for her beloved sister, Muriel Fagiani; and for the entire community of Napa. Together, these dedicated, skilled professionals diligently pursued the prosecution of this case, a prosecution that resulted in the conviction of serial killer Roy Melanson.

Proud detective Don Winegar with his wife and son following the new deputy sheriff's swearing-in ceremony. *Courtesy of Don Winegar.*

After Melanson's conviction in the Napa County Superior Court, his appeal was brought before the Court of Appeal of the State of California, First Appellate District Division Two. That court handed down its opinion on April 18, 2013. In its thirty-one-page decision, the court of appeal affirmed the judgment of the Napa County Superior Court. The judgment of life in prison for Roy Melanson became final.

AUTHOR'S NOTE

Identification of the victims has been disclosed where there has been publication of their identities in the record, newspapers, articles or books. In some cases, victims and their surviving family have passed on. However, identification of some of the persons has been disguised. These persons, whose families do not know what happened to them, will remain anonymous. I see no need to expose them here to painful memories or needless aggravation from either the unthinking or the malicious. To those who do not know them, their true names will not be significant to the drama in any case.

BIBLIOGRAPHY

Books

Jackson, Steve. *Smooth Talker*. Denver, CO: Wild Blue Press, 2015.
Shulman, Todd L. *Murder and Mayhem in the Napa Valley*. Charleston, SC: The History Press, 2012.

Articles

Napa Valley Register. "After 36 Years, Police Crack Brutal Slaying at Fagiani's Bar." December 31, 2010.
————. "Anita Andrews Was a Napa Type of Girl." March 21, 2010.
————. "Bar Customer Recalls Night of the Andrews Murder." September 22, 2011.
————. "Breaking the Code." March 22, 2010.
————. "Closure Comes to 37-Year-Old Fagiani Murder Case." December 29, 2011.
————. "Cops File 1974 Murder Case with DA's Office." June 17, 2010.
————. "DA Files Charges in 1974 Fagiani Bar Killing." July 21, 2010.
————. "End of the Trail?" June 19, 2001.
————. "Ex-Cops: Whoever Killed Andrews Probably Knew Her." July 11, 2004.
————. "Fagiani Murder Case Moves Closer to Trial." July 21, 2011.

———. "Fagiani Murder Trial Pushed to September." April 15, 2011.

———. "The Fagiani Sisters: Anita and Muriel." June 17, 2001.

———. "Fagiani's Bar Murder Ranks as Napa's Most Notorious Unsolved Crime." July 11, 2004.

———. "Fagiani's Bar Murder Trial Starts Monday." September 17, 2011.

———. "Fagiani's Murder: A Sigh of Relief…After 36 Years." January 20, 2010.

———. "Fagiani's Murder Suspect Implicated in Louisiana Killing." June 2, 2010.

———. "Fagiani's Sold, 33 Years after Murder: Napa Developer Buys Storied Main Street Property." December 15, 2007.

———. "Judge Supports Indictment in Fagiani Murder Case." August 9, 2011.

———. "Jury Begins Deliberations in Melanson Trial." September 29, 2011.

———. "Jury Hears Gruesome Testimony in Melanson Trial." September 27, 2011.

———. "Jury Selected in Melanson Murder Trial." September 20, 2011.

———. "Jury Visits Fagiani's Bar, Scene of 1974 Andrews Killing." September 23, 2011.

———. "A Long Time Coming: Former Investigators Elated by Break in 1974 Anita Andrews Case." January 25, 2010.

———. "Man Charged in 1974 Murder Extradited to Napa." September 11, 2010.

———. "Melanson Found Guilty of First-Degree Murder." September 30, 2011.

———. "Melanson Indicted in Fagiani's Murder." October 29, 2010.

———. "Melanson Jury Hears Openings, Police Testimony." September 21, 2011.

———. "Melanson Pleads Not Guilty in Killing at Fagiani's." September 16, 2010.

———. "The Murder at Fagiani's Bar." June 17, 2001.

———. "Muriel Fagiani, Napa's Most Concerned Citizen, Dies at Age 85." December 9, 2010.

———. "The Mystery on Main Street." March 21, 2010.

———. "Napa Police Plan to Seek Answers from DNA." June 19, 2001.

———. "Napa Readers Rank 2010's Top 10 Stories." January 4, 2011.

———. "Perseverance of Justice Is Without Limit." October 2, 2011.

———. "Police to Give a New Look at 10 Unsolved Murders." June 18, 2001.

———. "A Reporter's Notebook." March 22, 2010.

———. "Roy Melanson Timeline." March 21, 2010.

———. "Sides Rest in Melanson Murder Trial." September 28, 2011.

———. "Suspect in 1974 City Bar Murder Appears in Napa Court." September 14, 2010.

———. "Suspect in 36-Year-Old Fagiani's Cocktail Lounge Murder ID'd." January 18, 2010.

———. "Trial Date Set in Fagiani Case for May 9." November 19, 2010.

———. "Two Women May Share a Common Killer." March 22, 2010.

———. "What Happened the Night of July 10, 1974?" June 18, 2001.

———. "Witness Interviews to Be Recorded in 36-Year-Old Homicide." October 1, 2010.

———. "Woman Found Murdered in Family's Downtown Bar." July 11, 1974.

San Francisco Chronicle. "Napa Bar Is a Reminder of Old Murder." November 17, 1989.

St. Helena Star. "Recorded Fagiani Testimony Closed to Public." November 17, 2010.

Thill, John. "Fagiani's." Explore Napa, https://explorenapa.org/items/show/6.

ABOUT THE AUTHOR

Raymond A. Guadagni was the judge who presided over the Anita Andrews murder trial in 2011. Raised in Napa, California, he graduated from the University of California at Berkeley in 1968 and from Hastings College of Law in 1971. He practiced as a deputy public defender in Stockton, California, for three years before returning to his hometown in 1975 to establish a law practice. On November 1, 1995, Guadagni became Napa's first Superior Court Commissioner, and in 2001 he was appointed Superior Court Judge for the County of Napa. He retired in 2012 and is now an assigned judge with the Assigned Judges Program of California.

He is married with two adult daughters and five grandchildren. He enjoys babysitting his five grandchildren, writing, music and travel.